READING AND WRITING Sourcebook

Authors

Robert Pavlik

Richard G. Ramsey

Great Source Education Group

a Houghton Mifflin Company

Authors

Richard G. Ramsey is currently a national educational consultant for many schools throughout the country and serves as President of Ramsey's Communications. For more than twenty-three years he has served as a teacher and a principal for grades 1–12. Dr. Ramsey has also served on the Curriculum Frameworks Committee for the State of Florida. A lifelong teacher and educator and former principal, he is now a nationally known speaker on improving student achievement and motivating students.

Robert Pavlik taught high school English and reading for seven years. His university assignments in Colorado and Wisconsin have included teaching secondary/content area reading, chairing a Reading/Language Arts Department, and directing a Reading/Learning Center. He is an author of several books and articles and serves as the Director of the School Design and Development Center at Marquette University.

Table of Contents

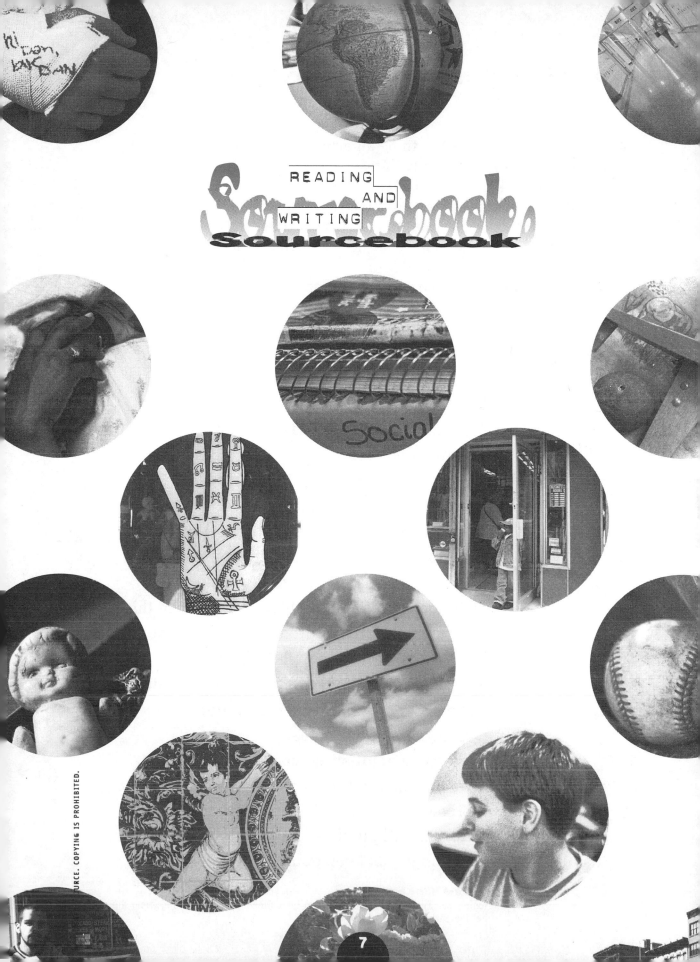

READING AND WRITING
Sourcebook

What does it mean to be an active reader and respond to literature? It means to read actively, with a pen in hand, and mark up the text. Active readers highlight parts they like and ones they'd like to reread. They take notes and write down their questions. Active readers also make a special point to think about how a reading connects to their life.

Read this poem. Notice how one reader has marked it up.

"How Things Work" by Gary Soto

RESPONSE NOTES

1. MARK OR HIGHLIGHT

Today it's going to cost us twenty dollars
To live. Five for a softball. Four for a book,
A handful of ones for coffee and two sweet rolls,

2. QUESTION
Why only $20?

Bus fare, rosin for your mother's violin.
We're completing our task. The tip I left
For the waitress filters down

3. CLARIFY
Tip gives life like rain.

Like rain, wetting the new roots of a child
Perhaps, a belligerent cat that won't let go

4. VISUALIZE

Of a balled sock until there's chicken to eat.
As far as I can tell, daughter, it works like this:
You buy bread from a grocery, a bag of apples
From a fruit stand, and what coins
Are passed on helps others buy pencils, glue,

5. PREDICT
He'll say $20 isn't enough money to live on.

Tickets to a movie in which laughter
Is thrown into their faces.
If we buy a goldfish, someone tries on a hat.
If we buy crayons, someone walks home with a broom.

6. REACT AND CONNECT
Sweet little poem about the way little things matter.

A tip, a small purchase here and there,
And things just keep going. I guess.

VOCABULARY
rosin—hard, yellow material made from turpentine used to keep things from slipping.
belligerent—fond of fighting.

Response Strategies

Active readers mark up texts in different ways. Every reader will mark or highlight different parts of a text, because each person sees and reacts to different words, phrases, and ideas. Here are 6 general strategies to use when responding to literature.

1. Mark or Highlight
With a pen or highlighter, underline or circle words that are important or seem confusing. By marking part of a text, you distinguish the important from the unimportant passages. That makes key parts easier to find when you need to reread or review.

2. Question
Ask yourself questions as you read: "Do I believe this?" or "Is this true?" Questions trigger thoughts in your mind and help make reading more meaningful.

3. Clarify
"What is the author trying to say? What does he or she mean?" Active readers are always trying to make clear what they have read. They often label, restate, or number parts of a text to keep track of what the author is saying.

4. Visualize
Active readers also draw pictures or make sketches as they read. Drawing or sketching helps readers remember the mental images they form when they read.

5. Predict
"How will this story end?" Active readers always make predictions as they read. Guessing what will come next helps them follow a story or article more closely and get more from their reading.

6. React and Connect
Active readers also write their opinions and comments in the margins of books or articles. This is another way readers can relate to what they're reading. It helps active readers understand their own views and make personal connections.

As you read this *Sourcebook*, use the response strategies and write in the Response Notes space.

Practice using some of the strategies with the selection below. Read the selection 2–3 times. Use a different response strategy each time you reread.

"Proving Myself" from *Your Move* by Eve Bunting

"You know the sign on the 405?" Kris asks me.

I don't know which sign he's talking about, but I nod anyway.

Isaac nods too, though he knows even less.

"The Snakes put their name on it," Kris says. "You're going up to put our name over theirs."

"Cool," I say, but I'm more nervous than ever.

I hold Isaac's hand as we cross the street; he tries to pull it away.

Now we're walking single file on the narrow road that borders the freeway. Above us traffic roars, loud as a thousand lawn mowers. We can't see it because there's a sloping bank with a wall on top. TV sounds blast from the houses we pass. A dog on a chain barks at us.

Kris stops and points.

High above the freeway, the green sign hangs on its metal pole. Two spotlights shine on it. ALTA EXIT it says. Except you can hardly see the words because SNAKES is written over them in red curvy letters.

My stomach is acting up. That sign is high. How am I supposed to get to it?

"James has to climb *that*?" Isaac asks. He's grabbing at my arms like he wants to keep me back. To tell the truth, I wish he could keep me back. I wish I could slink away. But how can I? I'm here to prove I'm tough enough to be in K-Bones.

Growing Up

Some of life's most important lessons take place during childhood. As we grow up, we make both mistakes and memories.

Believe it or not, one of the best ways to get ready to read is to write. Writing can help you think about a topic. It can also help you think about how the topic relates to your own life.

BEFORE YOU READ

Think of your childhood. Then think of a teacher or special person whom you remember well.

1. Do a 1-minute quickwrite describing this person.
2. Write everything you can think of. Be sure to describe how the person looks, sounds, and acts.

1-MINUTE QUICKWRITE

READ

Now read "Mrs. Olinski," part of a novel by E. L. Konigsburg.

1. **Mark** or **highlight** phrases and sentences that you think are important to understanding the characters.

2. Make notes about the characters in the Response Notes.

"Mrs. Olinski" from *The View from Saturday* by E. L. Konigsburg

Mrs. Olinski was the first teacher Epiphany ever had who taught from a wheelchair.
She sat, waiting, until we were all seated. Then she introduced herself. "I am Mrs. Olinski. I am one of those people who gets to use all those good parking spaces at the mall." She turned toward the blackboard and wrote in big, block letters:

MRS. OLINSKI
PARAPLEGIC

As she wrote *paraplegic*, Mrs. Olinski spelled it out, "P-A-R-A-P-L-E-G-I-C. It means that I am <u>paralyzed</u> from the waist down." Her voice was steady, but I noticed that her hands were not. The O of Olinski was not round or smooth but nervous. I don't know what made me look at Julian Singh at that moment, but I did. He sat upright in his chair, not looking at Mrs. Olinski or the blackboard but staring into the middle distance, as if looking at the word *paraplegic* or the paraplegic herself was too painful.

EXAMPLE:
She has a good
sense of humor!

VOCABULARY
paralyzed—unable to move or feel.

What do you know at this point about Mrs. Olinski?

....

....

....

Mrs. Olinski told us that she had become paralyzed in an automobile accident. Confined to a wheelchair as she was, she could not reach the top portion of the blackboard, so, stretch though she would, the words were written in the middle of the board— eye level for most standing sixth graders.

Hamilton Knapp, who had taken a seat in the very last row, farthest from the door, stood up and said, "Excuse me, Mrs. Olinski, but I can't see what you've written. Could you write a little higher on the blackboard, please?"

Mrs. Olinski smiled. "Not at the moment," she said.

Ham sat down and said, "Sorry." She didn't mean that smile, and Ham Knapp didn't mean that "sorry."

The remainder of the morning was taken up with bookkeeping matters such as passing out supplies and assigning seats. We were seated in alphabetical order, and as luck would have it, Ham Knapp ended up way back in the room, in the very seat he had chosen for himself.

Nadia Diamondstein was seated three rows over and two rows forward. I could see her red hair. Nadia and I were almost related. This

VOCABULARY
Confined—restricted.
bookkeeping—work of keeping records.

14

"Mrs. Olinski" continued

What 2 or 3 things have happened so far in the story?

....

....

....

RESPONSE NOTES

past summer, her grandfather had married my grandmother. In August when I visited them, Nadia was visiting her father. We often walked the beach together. And one day after a storm, we rescued a batch of <u>hatchling</u> turtles and took them out to sea.

The light from the window shone on Nadia's side of the room. When she moved her head, the morning light caught in her hair the way the sun had when she turned her back to the ocean. <u>Fringes</u> of her hair framed her face in a halo. Whenever that halo effect happened, I wanted to stare at her until the sunlight stopped, but my heart stopped before the light did. Then there was a period during my vacation when Nadia chose not to walk with her father and me. I waited for her to catch up, and when I did, she slowed down, and I missed seeing the light in her hair. I never told Nadia how much I liked seeing the halo the sunlight made of her hair. Sometimes silence is a habit that hurts.

Noah Gershom sat in back of Michael Froelich and in front of Hamilton Knapp. His father is our family dentist. His mother sells houses—a lot of them in The Farm—and for

VOCABULARY
hatchling—young.
Fringes—threads hanging loose.

reasons too complicated to tell, Noah Gershom was best man at my grandmother Draper's wedding early last summer. It was pretty funny the way it happened, but my mother, who was maid of honor, was not amused. She cannot forgive Mrs. Gershom for selling houses at The Farm. I think she would change dentists if there were another one as good in Epiphany. Potters have always taken good care of their land and their teeth.

Julian Singh sat in the row to my right and two seats back.

At lunch time, I sat on the end of the bench. Noah took a seat next to me. Nadia came from the food line carrying her tray and found no vacant seat at any of the girls' tables, so she sat next to Noah. Julian, who had brought his lunch, was seated at a table at the far end of the room, all alone. He finished eating and left the cafeteria without waiting for the bell or asking permission. When Mrs. Olinski saw him leave, she followed. She must have wanted to tell him the rules without calling him out to embarrass him. It took her a while to <u>maneuver</u> her wheelchair between the tables, so Julian had a head start. Shortly after Mrs. Olinski made her way through the door, the bell did ring, and we all left, and were just behind Mrs. Olinski as she made her way down the hall.

When we entered the classroom, we saw that someone had erased PARAPLEGIC and

VOCABULARY
maneuver—move.

written CRIPPLE instead. Julian was the only person in the room. He was facing the blackboard, holding an eraser. He turned around, looking startled when he saw us file in, led by Mrs. Olinski in her wheelchair.

STOP AND THINK

What happened in Mrs. Olinski's room at lunch time?

....

....

Mrs. Olinski approached him wordlessly. She held out her hand, and Julian silently handed over the eraser. Mrs. Olinski turned from him to the blackboard and slowly and deliberately erased the word CRIPPLE.

The question was: Had Julian erased PARAPLEGIC, or was he in the process of erasing CRIPPLE? I glanced back at Hamilton Knapp and saw him exchange a look and a slight smile with Michael Froelich, and I knew the answer.

VOCABULARY
CRIPPLE—offensive word meaning disabled.
startled—surprised; shocked.
deliberately—intentionally or on purpose.
glanced—quickly looked.

STOP AND RETELL STOP AND RETELL STOP AND RETELL

Use this sequence organizer to show what happens first, what happens next, and what happens after that.

1.	2.	3.

NARROW YOUR FOCUS When you write about a person, you don't need to tell *everything*. You zoom in on the most important parts. This is called narrowing your focus.

1. Think about 5 people you remember well from growing up. Look back at your quickwrite on page 12. They may be relatives, teachers, or any persons special to you. Write their names in the boxes.

2. Then narrow your focus. Choose 1 person to describe in a paragraph. Put his or her name in the large box.

3. Write 3 reasons this person was special to you when you were growing up.

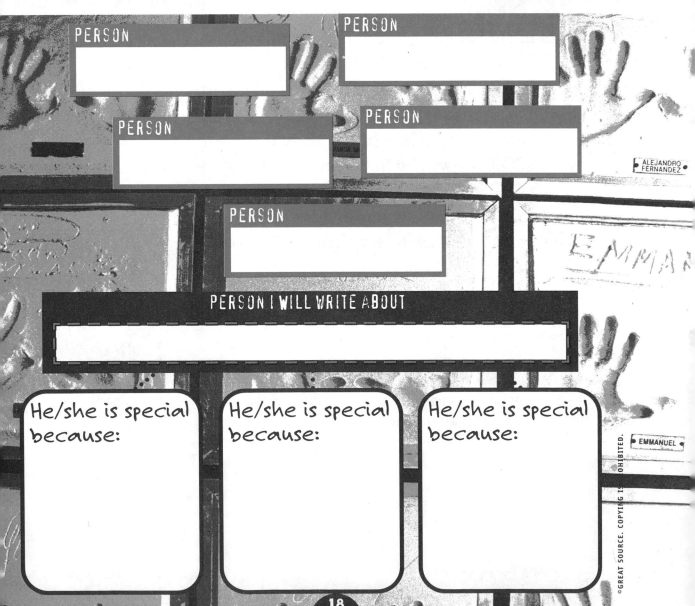

PERSON

PERSON

PERSON

PERSON

PERSON

PERSON I WILL WRITE ABOUT

He/she is special because:

He/she is special because:

He/she is special because:

IV. WRITE

Write a **paragraph** describing the special person from your organizer.

1. Include 3 or more details that help your readers understand why this person stands out in your mind.

2. When you've finished, use the Writers' Checklist to help you revise.

WRITERS' CHECKLIST

SENTENCES

☐ Did all of your sentences begin with capital letters and end with the correct punctuation (a period, an exclamation point, or a question mark)?
EXAMPLES: *What is this story about? She's so excited to read it! I hope it's funny.*

☐ Did every sentence express a complete thought? EXAMPLES: *Mrs. Olinski erasing.* (Incomplete) *Mrs. Olinski was erasing the board.* (Complete)

In your own words, what is the main idea of "Mrs. Olinski"?

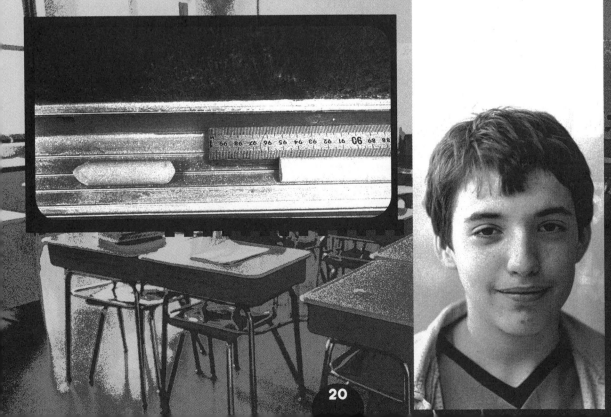

2: The Day It Rained Cockroaches

Can it really rain cockroaches? The author Paul Zindel might say it can. He might also tell you that one of the reasons to read is to learn things about ourselves and our world.

I. BEFORE YOU READ

Get in a group with 2-3 students. Choose a reader to begin. Have the reader read the story's title and opening paragraph.

1. Listen carefully. Try to visualize—that is, see in your mind—what the author describes.
2. Complete the Listener's Guide below.

DIRECTIONS Answer each question as best as you can. If you don't know an answer, leave it blank.

WHERE DOES THE STORY TAKE PLACE?

WHEN DOES IT TAKE PLACE?

WHO ARE THE CHARACTERS?

WHAT WILL THE STORY BE ABOUT?

LISTENER'S GUIDE

Now listen as a classmate reads the rest of this selection from the novel *The Pigman and Me.*

1. As you listen, **visualize** the people and places he describes.

2. Make sketches of what you "see" in the Response Notes.

RESPONSE NOTES

EXAMPLE:

"The Day It Rained Cockroaches" from *The Pigman and Me* by Paul Zindel

When we first drove into the town, I noticed a lot of plain wood houses, a Catholic church, a war memorial, three <u>saloons</u> with men sitting outside on chairs, seventeen women wearing <u>kerchiefs</u> on their heads, a one-engine firehouse, a big redbrick school, a candy store, and a butcher shop with about 300 sausages hanging in the window. Betty shot me a private look, signaling she was <u>aghast</u>. Travis was mainly a Polish town, and was so special-looking that, years later, it was picked as a location for filming the movie *Splendor in the Grass*, which starred Natalie Wood (before she drowned), and Warren Beatty (before he dated Madonna). Travis was selected because they needed a town that looked like it was Kansas in 1920, which it still looks like.

The address of our new home was 123 Glen Street. We stopped in front, and for a few moments the house looked normal: brown shingles, pea-soup-green painted sides, a tiny

VOCABULARY
saloons—taverns; bars.
kerchiefs—square scarves.
aghast—shocked; amazed.

yellow porch, untrimmed hedges, and a <u>rickety</u> wood gate and fence. Across the street to the left was a slope with worn gravestones all over it. The best-<u>preserved</u> ones were at the top, peeking out of patches of poison oak.

The backyard of our house was an airport. I mean, the house had two acres of land of its own, but beyond the rear fence was a huge field consisting of a single dirt runway, lots of old propeller-driven Piper Cub-type planes, and a cluster of rusted <u>hangars</u>. This was the most <u>underprivileged</u> airport I'd ever seen, bordered on its west side by the Arthur Kill channel and on its south side by a Con Edison electric power plant with big black mountains of coal. The only great sight was a huge apple tree on the far left corner of our property. Its trunk was at least three feet wide. It had strong, thick branches rich with new, flapping leaves. It reached upward like a giant's hand grabbing for the sky.

"Isn't everything beautiful?" Mother beamed.

"Yes, Mom," I said.

Betty gave me a pinch for lying.

"I'll plant my own rose garden," Mother went on, fumbling for the key. "Lilies, tulips, violets!"

VOCABULARY
rickety—shaky; likely to fall apart.
preserved—maintained; kept.
hangars—shelters for housing or repairing aircrafts.
underprivileged—unfortunate.

Mom opened the front door and we went inside. We were so excited, we ran through the echoing empty rooms, pulling up old, <u>soiled</u> shades to let the sunlight crash in. We ran upstairs and downstairs, all over the place like wild ponies. The only unpleasant thing, from my point of view, was that we weren't the only ones running around. There were a lot of cockroaches <u>scurrying</u> from our invading footfalls and the <u>shafts</u> of light.

STOP AND ORGANIZE

Use this organizer to show what you know so far about "The Day It Rained Cockroaches."

WHO IS INVOLVED?

WHEN DOES THE STORY TAKE PLACE?

STOP AND ORGANIZE

"Yes, the house has a few roaches," Mother confessed. "We'll get rid of them in no time!"

"How?" Betty asked raising an eyebrow.

"I bought eight Gulf Insect Bombs!"

"Where are they?" I asked.

Mother dashed out to the car and came back with one of the suitcases. From it she spilled the bombs, which looked like big silver <u>hand grenades</u>.

VOCABULARY
soiled—stained.
scurrying—running.
shafts—rays.
hand grenades—hand-held containers that explode when smashed.

"We just put one in each room and turn them on!" Mother explained.

She took one of the bombs, set it in the middle of the upstairs kitchen, and turned on its nozzle. A cloud of gas began to stream from it, and we hurried into the other rooms to set off the other bombs.

"There!" Mother said. "Now we have to get out!"

"Get out?" I coughed.

"Yes. We must let the poison fill the house for four hours before we can come back in! Lucky for us there's a Lassie double feature playing at the Ritz!"

We hadn't been in the house ten minutes before we were driving off again!

I suppose you might as well know now that my mother really *loved* Lassie movies. The only thing she enjoyed more were movies in which romantic couples got killed at the end by tidal waves, volcanoes, or other natural disasters. Anyway, I was glad we were gassing the roaches, because they are the one insect I despise. Tarantulas I like. Scorpions I can live with. But ever since I was three years old and my mother took me to a World's Fair, I have had nightmares about cockroaches. Most people remember an exciting water ride this fair had called the Shoot-the-Chutes, but emblazoned on my brain is the display the fair featured of giant, live African cockroaches,

VOCABULARY

nozzle—projecting part with an opening.
Lassie double feature—showing of two Lassie movies in a row.
despise—dislike.
emblazoned—marked.

which look like American cockroaches except they're six inches long, have furry legs, and can pinch flesh. In my nightmares about them, I'm usually lying on a bed in a dark room and I notice a bevy of giant cockroaches heading for me. I try to run away but find out that someone has secretly tied me down on the bed, and the African roaches start crawling up the sides of the sheets. They walk all over my body, and then they head for my face. When they start trying to drink from my mouth is when I wake up screaming.

So after the movie I was actually looking forward to going back to the house and seeing all the dead cockroaches.

"Wasn't Lassie wonderful?" Mother sighed as she drove us back to Travis. "The way that brave dog was able to crawl hundreds of miles home after being kidnapped and beaten by Nazi Secret Service Police!"

"Yes, Mom," I agreed, although I was truthfully tired of seeing a dog movie star keep pulling the same set of tear-jerking stunts in each of its movies.

VOCABULARY

bevy—group.
Nazi Secret Service Police—the undercover division of the Nazi police force when Hitler ruled as dictator of Germany.

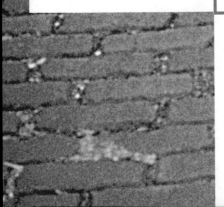

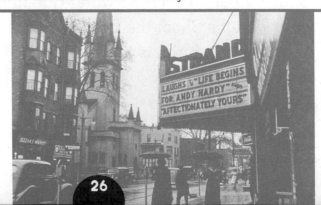

26

"The Day It Rained Cockroaches" continued

WHERE DOES THE STORY TAKE PLACE?

WHAT IS THE PROBLEM?

STOP AND ORGANIZE
RESPONSE NOTES

"Maybe we'll get a dog just like Lassie one day," Mother sighed.

When we got back to the house this time, we didn't run into it. We walked inside very slowly, sniffing for the deadly gas. I didn't care about the gas so much as I wanted to see a lot of roach <u>corpses</u> all over the place so I'd be able to sleep in peace.

But there were none.

"Where are all the dead roaches?" I asked.

"I don't know," Mother admitted.

We crept slowly upstairs to see if the bodies might be there. I knew the kitchen had the most roaches, but when we went in, I didn't see a single one, living or dead. The lone empty Gulf Insect Bomb sat <u>spent</u> in the middle of the floor. My sister picked up the bomb and started reading the directions. One thing my mother never did was follow directions. As Betty was reading, I noticed a closed closet

VOCABULARY
corpses—dead bodies.
spent—used up; empty.

RESPONSE NOTES

door and reached out to turn its knob.

"It says here we should've opened all the closet doors before setting off the bombs, so roaches can't hide." Betty moaned, her clue to me that Mom had messed up again.

I had already started to open the door. My mind knew what was going to happen, but it was too late to tell my hand to stop pulling on the door. It sprang open, and suddenly, 5,000 very angry, living cockroaches rained down on me from the ceiling of the closet.

"Eeehhhhhh!" I screamed, leaping around the room, bathed in bugs, slapping at the roaches crawling all over me and down my neck! "Eeehhhhhh! Eeehh! Ehhh! Ehh!"

"Don't worry. I'll get more bombs," Mother said comfortingly as she grabbed an old dishrag to knock the <u>fluttering</u> roaches off my back. Betty calmly reached out her foot to crunch as many as dared run by her.

STOP AND ORGANIZE

WHAT HAPPENS AT THE END?

HOW IS THE PROBLEM SOLVED?

STOP AND ORGANIZE

STOP AND ORGANIZE

STOP AND ORGANIZE

VOCABULARY
fluttering—flapping.

III. GATHER YOUR THOUGHTS

CONNECT Get ready to write a narrative paragraph.
1. Think of a time something funny happened to you or your family when you were growing up.
2. Make notes about the event in the boxes.

WHO WAS INVOLVED?

WHEN DID IT TAKE PLACE?

WHERE DID IT TAKE PLACE?

WHAT WAS THE PROBLEM?

WHAT HAPPENED?

HOW WAS THE PROBLEM SOLVED?

IV. WRITE

Write a **narrative paragraph** about something that happened when you were growing up.

1. Give plenty of details so that your reader can "see" the events you are describing.

2. Use the Writers' Checklist to help you revise.

V. WRAP-UP

What did "The Day It Rained Cockroaches" mean to you?

Colonial America

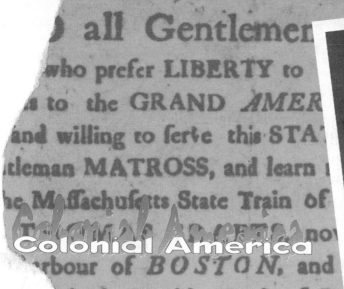

Before the United States was a free world power, it was a controlled British colony. The Boston Tea Party of 1773 was one of the first demonstrations of America's call for freedom. It took a year of fighting the British in the Revolutionary War, however, before America declared its independence in 1776.

3: Eyewitness to the Boston Tea Party

Let's say you are looking for information about the American Revolution. Your library probably has about 312 books on this subject. Will you read every one? No, you'll skim through several, looking for answers to your questions.

I. BEFORE YOU READ

Suppose you wanted to answer this one question: What is "Eyewitness to the Boston Tea Party" about?

1. Now skim the selection. Watch especially for names, dates, places, and phrases that catch your eye.

2. Note what you find in the boxes below. Then answer the question at the bottom of the page.

KEY WORDS AND PHRASES

NAMES OF PEOPLE

NAMES OF PLACES

DATES

INTERESTING PHRASES

Who and what is "Eyewitness to the Boston Tea Party" about?

II. READ

Now carefully and slowly read "Eyewitness to the Boston Tea Party."
1. **Clarify** the main events described.
2. Write important details about the Boston Tea Party in the Response Notes.

"Eyewitness to the Boston Tea Party"
by Wesley S. Griswold

RESPONSE NOTES

The raiders were <u>predominantly</u> young. Only seven of them were over forty. Of those whose age at the time could later be determined, sixteen were in their thirties, thirty-eight were in their twenties, and fifteen were teen-agers. The youngest <u>contingent</u> consisted entirely of <u>apprentices</u>. They had not been taken into consideration when the plans were being laid. Unable to resist the <u>allure</u> of whistles and <u>warwhoops</u> in the street, they simply joined the Party on the spur of the moment, <u>for a lark</u>. Most of them were not disguised. Indeed, many of the older men were only partially so, having done no more than discolor their faces.

The decision had apparently been made at the secret session of the Committees of Correspondence from five towns held in <u>Faneuil Hall</u> on December 13th to have three groups of men, including the leaders of the raid, <u>don makeshift Indian attire</u> for the occasion. It was truly a crude disguise, consisting mostly of

EXAMPLE:
Most who took part were young.

VOCABULARY
predominantly—mostly.
contingent—group of troops.
apprentices—beginners.
allure—attraction.
warwhoops—loud shouts or yells.
for a lark—on a whim.
Faneuil Hall—a meeting place in Boston, Massachusetts.
don makeshift Indian attire—wear clothes like Native Americans wear.

RESPONSE NOTES

ragged clothes, any sort of hood for the head and shoulders, and some <u>obscuring</u> color for the face and hands. Headgear included blankets, shawls, cast-off dresses, and red woolen caps. Skin colors ranged from red <u>ochre</u>, through a mixture of that <u>pigment with lampblack</u> and axle grease, to pure soot. If anyone wore a feathered headband, no <u>contemporary</u> account mentioned it.

stop and think

What are the disguises for?

....

....

The three groups <u>assembled</u> in separate parts of town and began putting on their costumes and makeup during the short afternoon of December 16th. . . . By dark, they were ready to make their way to a designated <u>rendezvous</u> on Fort Hill. . . .

. . .Robert Sessions, writing in his old age, provided particularly vivid recollections of the scene:

I was living in Boston at the time, in the family of a Mr. Davis, a lumber merchant, as a common laborer. On that eventful evening, when Mr. Davis

VOCABULARY
obscuring—darkening.
ochre—reddish clay mixture.
pigment with lampblack—color that uses fine black soot (the lampblack) that comes from burning oil in lamps.
contemporary—current.
assembled—gathered.
rendezvous—meeting point.

"Eyewitness to the Boston Tea Party" CONTINUED

came in from the town meeting, I asked him what was to be done with the tea.

"They are now throwing it overboard," he replied.

Receiving permission, I went immediately to the spot. Everything was as light as day, by the means of lamps and torches; a pin might be seen lying on the wharf. I went on board where they were at work, and took hold with my own hands.

stop and think

Who is telling this story?

_____

_____

I was not one of those appointed to destroy the tea, and who disguised themselves as Indians, but was a volunteer, the disguised men being largely men of family and position in Boston, while I was a young man whose home and relations were in Connecticut. The appointed and disguised party proving too small for the quick work necessary, other young men, similarly circumstanced with myself, joined them in their labors.

The chests were drawn up by a tackle—one man bringing them forward [in the hold], another putting a rope around them, and others hoisting them to the deck and carrying them to the vessel's side. The chests were then opened, the tea emptied over the side, and the chests thrown overboard.

VOCABULARY
wharf—pier where ships load and unload.
similarly circumstanced—sharing the same situation (in this case, being unknown and not from the Boston area).
tackle—rope.
hoisting—lifting.
vessel's—ship's.

RESPONSE NOTES

Perfect regularity <u>prevailed</u> during the whole transaction. Although there were many people on the wharf, entire silence prevailed—no clamor, no talking. Nothing was <u>meddled</u> with but the teas on board.

After having emptied the whole, the deck was swept clean, and everything put in its proper place. An officer on board was requested to come up from the cabin and see that no damage was done except to the tea. . . .

VOCABULARY
prevailed—won out.
meddled—bothered; disturbed.

stop and think

What was the purpose of the "tea party"?

....

....

....

Was the party wild and out-of-control or peaceful and orderly? How do you know?

....

....

....

III. GATHER YOUR THOUGHTS

A. RETELL Robert Sessions was an eyewitness to the Boston Tea Party. Write 1–2 sentences that describe what he saw.

B. DESCRIBE Think of an interesting event that you eyewitnessed. Get ready to write a letter about it.
1. List facts about the event in the top box.
2. Then write 3 details you'd want to include in a letter describing the event to a friend.

MAIN IDEA

WHAT:

WHERE:

WHEN:

DETAIL 1:

DETAIL 2:

DETAIL 3:

IV. WRITE

Write a **letter** to a friend describing the event you saw.
1. Include information from your organizer.
2. Use the Writers' Checklist when it is time to revise.

date

greeting

closing

V. WRAP-UP

Did you find "Eyewitness to the Boston Tea Party" easy or hard to read? Why?

4: Lexington and Concord

As a reader, you never come to a selection empty-handed. You bring with you information, ideas, and feelings that you've gathered over the years. This knowledge helps you understand what you read.

BEFORE YOU READ

Complete the K-W-L Chart below.

1. In the **K** column, write anything you know about Paul Revere and his famous ride.
2. In the **W** column, write what you want to find out. Save the **L** column for later.

K-W-L CHART

K What I Know	**W** What I Want to Know	**L** What I Learned
EXAMPLE: Revere rode a horse.	Where was he coming from?	

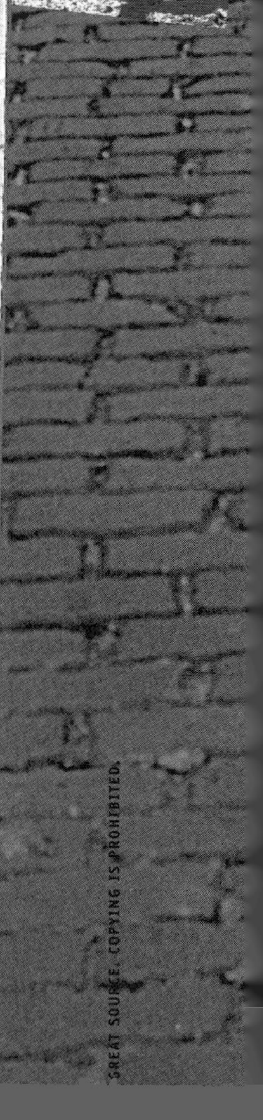

READ

I. Now read "Lexington and Concord."

1. As you read, think about what the author's main idea is.

2. Record your **questions** about important people and events in the Response Notes.

"Lexington and Concord" by Bruce Bliven, Jr.

RESPONSE NOTES

General Gage was a <u>mild</u>, <u>moderate</u> man whose wife was American. He had seized the Americans' gunpowder because it was his duty as a British officer to make sure that rebels were in no position to <u>resist</u> the British government. He hoped there would be no trouble, but when his spies reported that the Americans had <u>stores of arms and ammunition</u> at Concord, about eighteen miles from Boston, Gage knew it was his duty to take those weapons away.

The General wanted to surprise Concord, but it was impossible for the British army in Boston to keep secrets. Because the port was closed, the city was full of Bostonians with no jobs who had time to watch every move the British made and report it to the Boston Committee.

On the night of April 18, 1775, Dr. Joseph Warren, head of the Boston Committee, sent for his two best express riders, William Dawes and Paul Revere. He told them the British were sending out troops that night. The <u>redcoats</u> were to march to Lexington to arrest John Hancock and Sam Adams, who were staying there. Then

EXAMPLE:
How long a ride was it?

VOCABULARY
mild—gentle; kind.
moderate—reasonable.
resist—work against.
stores of arms and ammunition—extra supplies of guns and bullets.
redcoats—British soldiers.

RESPONSE NOTES

they were to go on to Concord to seize the Americans' stock of weapons. The riders had to get a warning through the circle of British roadblocks around Boston.

STOP AND PREDICT

Which rider do you think will be successful in delivering the warning—Dawes or Revere?

Dawes galloped off on one road and slipped past the British <u>sentries</u> in the dark by falling in with some soldiers who happened to be passing the guard post. Revere, after telling an <u>associate</u> to set two signal lanterns in the steeple of the Old North Church, was rowed quietly across the river to Charlestown. There, friends who had seen the lights were waiting with a horse, and away he galloped.

Revere, who had the shorter road, got to Lexington first. Adams and Hancock were bundled off to safety, and the Lexington <u>militia</u>, about 130 men commanded by Captain Jonas Parker, turned out on the village green.

It was four-thirty in the morning before the British appeared. By then nearly half of Parker's men had gone home. The rest—perhaps 70 men in all—formed two lines on the green. They watched, <u>dismayed</u>, while the advance guard of

VOCABULARY

sentries—guards, especially soldiers.
associate—companion; partner.
militia—army of ordinary citizens.
dismayed—frightened.

"Lexington and Concord" CONTINUED

more than 600 British soldiers, in brilliant red and white with gleaming brass buttons and buckles, moved on the double from their <u>column</u> of march into a battle line.

"Stand your ground!" Captain Parker shouted.

"Don't fire unless fired upon. But if they want to have a war, let it begin here!"

And here it began.

Captain Parker, after a moment, realized the hopeless position of his tiny force. Knowing that Adams and Hancock were already safe, he ordered his men to <u>disband</u>.

But the British commander, Major Pitcairn, had orders to disarm the Americans, and he wanted their guns.

STOP AND PREDICT

Will Parker's men give up their guns or fight?

....

....

....

"Lay down your arms, you rebels!" the major shouted.

There was a single shot, then an order to fire given by some British officer—not Major Pitcairn—and a <u>platoon volley</u> over the heads of the Americans. A second British volley killed Captain Parker. Before the fight ended—if the few scattered shots returned by the Lexington

VOCABULARY
column—line of soldiers.
disband—break from the group.
platoon volley—mass firing.

RESPONSE NOTES

men could be called a fight—seven other Americans were killed and ten more were wounded.

As the sun rose, the British marched on to Concord. The men of the town had worked all night hiding the military stores from the British. Now they waited in front of Concord for the soldiers to come.

Seeing the overwhelming size of the British column, however, the 150 local militiamen beat a retreat. They withdrew through their town, across North Bridge, a small farm bridge over the Concord River, and took posts on high ground beyond it.

The British spent the morning searching, with little success, for the hidden guns and ammunition. They accidentally set fire to the courthouse and a blacksmith shop, but quickly put out the flames.

Meanwhile help for the Concord militia was on the way. Every town nearby had heard the church bells ringing an alarm, and militiamen, hurrying to pick up their muskets, formed into squads and marched to the scene. By the time the smoke rose from the fires in Concord, three or four hundred Americans, including reinforcements from Acton, Bedford and Lincoln, were there.

VOCABULARY

stores—supplies.
muskets—guns.
Acton, Bedford and Lincoln—cities in the colony of Massachusetts.

"Lexington and Concord" CONTINUED

The Americans, thinking the British were burning Concord, decided to reenter the town "or die in the attempt." For two or three minutes the British and the militiamen fired at each other across the North Bridge, and several men on both sides were killed.

STOP AND PREDICT

RESPONSE NOTES

Who will win the battle at Concord—the British or the Americans? Why?

....

....

....

The British <u>retreated</u> into Concord and got ready to march back to Boston. The Americans, strengthened every few minutes by the arrival of a new company of militia, prepared to fight a strange battle, a series of <u>flank attacks</u> and <u>ambushes</u> on the British column as it marched along the road. It was a nightmare for the redcoats, drilled to fight in <u>formal formations</u>. The Americans, who fired on the marchers and then hurried ahead to take up new positions and fire again, seemed to be everywhere; flashes of musket fire blazed at the British from houses, barns, from behind stone walls and trees. British casualties were heavy.

By the time the British column reached Lexington, the running fight had turned into a

VOCABULARY
retreated—moved back in defeat.
flank attacks—attacks from the side.
ambushes—sudden attacks made from a hidden location.
formal formations—battle lines in which one army faces another.

rout. The redcoats were badly disorganized. If the Americans had been an army instead of small volunteer units rushing to the scene of action, the British force might have been wiped out.

But a British rescue party of 1,000 soldiers was on the way. General Gage had guessed that, in spite of his hopes, there might be trouble for his expedition. And though the Americans continued to attack along the entire sixteen-mile route back to Boston, especially near the towns of Arlington and Cambridge, the fresh body of British troops with additional artillery prevented the defeat from being worse than it was. The British lost 273 men either killed, wounded or missing—more than twice as many as the Americans.

As the British force reached the safety of Boston after sunset, a ring of Massachusetts militiamen closed in around the city. In a matter of days, militiamen from all the neighboring colonies marched in to join the Massachusetts men. Ten thousand recruits surrounded Boston, blockading it from the land—just as the British had blockaded it by sea.

VOCABULARY
rout—disorderly fight.
expedition—march; journey.
artillery—weapons.
blockading—blocking; isolating.

Now that you have finished reading, go back to the K-W-L Chart on page 40 and fill in the **L** (What I Learned) column.

"Lexington and Concord" CONTINUED

The Americans, thinking the British were burning Concord, decided to reenter the town "or die in the attempt." For two or three minutes the British and the militiamen fired at each other across the North Bridge, and several men on both sides were killed.

STOP AND PREDICT

Who will win the battle at Concord—the British or the Americans? Why?

....

....

....

The British <u>retreated</u> into Concord and got ready to march back to Boston. The Americans, strengthened every few minutes by the arrival of a new company of militia, prepared to fight a strange battle, a series of <u>flank attacks</u> and <u>ambushes</u> on the British column as it marched along the road. It was a nightmare for the redcoats, drilled to fight in <u>formal formations</u>. The Americans, who fired on the marchers and then hurried ahead to take up new positions and fire again, seemed to be everywhere; flashes of musket fire blazed at the British from houses, barns, from behind stone walls and trees. British casualties were heavy.

By the time the British column reached Lexington, the running fight had turned into a

VOCABULARY

retreated—moved back in defeat.
flank attacks—attacks from the side.
ambushes—sudden attacks made from a hidden location.
formal formations—battle lines in which one army faces another.

rout. The redcoats were badly disorganized. If the Americans had been an army instead of small volunteer units rushing to the scene of action, the British force might have been wiped out.

But a British rescue party of 1,000 soldiers was on the way. General Gage had guessed that, in spite of his hopes, there might be trouble for his expedition. And though the Americans continued to attack along the entire sixteen-mile route back to Boston, especially near the towns of Arlington and Cambridge, the fresh body of British troops with additional artillery prevented the defeat from being worse than it was. The British lost 273 men either killed, wounded or missing—more than twice as many as the Americans.

As the British force reached the safety of Boston after sunset, a ring of Massachusetts militiamen closed in around the city. In a matter of days, militiamen from all the neighboring colonies marched in to join the Massachusetts men. Ten thousand recruits surrounded Boston, blockading it from the land—just as the British had blockaded it by sea.

VOCABULARY
rout—disorderly fight.
expedition—march; journey.
artillery—weapons.
blockading—blocking; isolating.

Now that you have finished reading, go back to the K-W-L Chart on page 40 and fill in the **L** (What I Learned) column.

©GREAT SOURCE. COPYING IS PROHIBITED.

GATHER YOUR THOUGHTS

A. WRITE A TOPIC SENTENCE Get ready to write a summary of "Lexington and Concord." First write a topic sentence that tells what the paragraph is about.

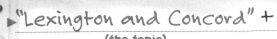

"Lexington and Concord" +

(the topic)   (what the author says about it)

=

your topic sentence

B. LIST DETAILS Now make a list of 3-4 details that support your topic sentence. Use the example as a model.

YOUR TOPIC SENTENCE AND DETAILS

TOPIC SENTENCE:

DETAIL #1

DETAIL #2

DETAIL #3

EXAMPLE

TOPIC SENTENCE: "Eyewitness to the Boston Tea Party" is a vivid account of what happened on that famous night.

DETAIL #1 The author describes the men and their disguises.

DETAIL #2 He explains how the men dumped the tea.

DETAIL #3 He tells what happened afterwards.

For their Encouragement
Bounty on paſsing Muſter,

IV. WRITE

Write a **summary** of "Lexington and Concord."

1. Use your topic sentence as your first sentence.

2. Then write your details. Start a new sentence for each detail.

3. Refer to the Writers' Checklist when you revise.

V. WRAP-UP

What did you like best about "Lexington and Concord"?

Esther Forbes

CONCORD

LEXINGTON

MYSTIC RIVER

Paul Revere's Ride

CAMBRIDGE

BUNKER HILL

OLD NORTH CHURCH

BOSTON

BOSTON HARBOR

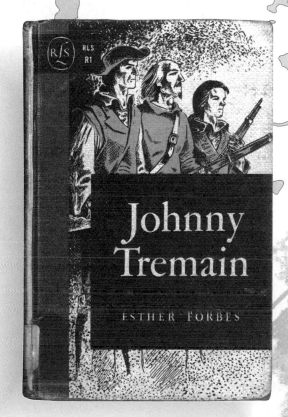

RLS R1

Johnny Tremain

ESTHER FORBES

Esther Forbes (1891–1967) won the 1943 Pulitzer Prize for her biography, *Paul Revere and the World He Lived In*. It was then that she became inspired to write more about the events surrounding the Revolutionary War. Her novel *Johnny Tremain* won the Newbery Medal in 1944.

5: Ready

Imagine you're going to the store to buy a present for a friend. Will you rush into the store and buy the first thing you see? No, you'll take the time to walk through the store and look around. The same is true for reading. Good readers walk through a story or article before they read it.

I. BEFORE YOU READ

Walk through "Ready," a part of the novel *Johnny Tremain*.

1. Glance through the first and the last paragraphs of the selection.

2. Then skim the rest of the selection. Look for names of characters and places. Make notes about what catches your eye.

Walk-Through

WHO IS THE AUTHOR?

WHAT IS THE TITLE OF THE STORY?

WHAT CHARACTER NAMES DID YOU NOTICE?

WHAT PLACE NAMES DID YOU NOTICE?

WHAT ELSE CAUGHT YOUR EYE?

WHAT DO YOU THINK THE STORY IS ABOUT?

II. READ

Now read "Ready."

1. As you read, think about what the characters do and say.

2. Write your **predictions** about the characters in the Response Notes.

"Ready" from *Johnny Tremain* by Esther Forbes

All day one could feel something was <u>afoot</u>. Johnny read it on Colonel Smith's <u>florid</u> face. He was stepping across the Queen's stable yard very <u>briskly</u> and remembering to pull in his <u>paunch</u>. There was ardor in his eye. Was it <u>martial ardor</u>?

Lieutenant Stranger was so happy over something he gave Dove <u>threepence</u>.

Spring had come unreasonably early this year. In the yard of the Africa Queen, peach trees were already in blossom. Stranger was so happy something was bound to happen. Over on the <u>Common</u> Johnny found Earl Percy's <u>regiment</u> <u>unlimbering</u>, polishing two cannons. The soldiers were forming a <u>queue</u> about a <u>grindstone</u> sharpening their bayonets. What of it? They were always doing things like that. Did all this mean something or nothing?

He went to Mr. Revere's, whose wife told him to look for him at Doctor Warren's. The two friends sat in the surgery making their plans

EXAMPLE:
Johnny will end up doing something dangerous.

VOCABULARY

afoot—in progress.
florid—flushed; reddish.
briskly—quickly.
paunch—large stomach.
martial ardor—strong feeling; war-like intensity.
threepence—a small amount of money or change, like a tip.
Common—short for Boston Common, a park and gathering place.
regiment—military unit of ground troops.
unlimbering—preparing for action.
queue—line.
grindstone—hard stone used for sharpening knives, scissors, and so forth.

and listening to reports that were coming from all directions. Seemingly the excitement among the officers, the preparations among the soldiers, had been noticed by at least a dozen others. But where were they going? Who would command them? No one knew. Possibly only Gage himself, although before the start was actually made he would have to tell his officers.

stop+predict

What do you think Johnny Tremain will have to do?

....

....

stop+predict

All that day the British transports had been readying their landing boats. This might mean men would be taken aboard, move off down the coast (as Salem had been invaded two months before), or that they were standing by merely to ferry the men across the Charles River, land them in Charlestown or Cambridge. The work on the boats suggested that the men would not march out through the town gates. And yet . . . Gage might have ordered this work done merely to confuse the people of Boston. Blind them to his real direction. The talk at Doctor Warren's went on into the night.

Johnny relaxed on a sofa in the surgery as the men talked. He was ready to run wherever sent, find out any fact for them. It was past midnight. He would not have known he had been asleep except that he had been

VOCABULARY
merely—only.
ferry—carry.

"Ready" continued

dreaming. He had been hard at work down on Hancock's Wharf boiling lobsters—he and John Hancock and Sam Adams. The lobsters had men's eyes with long lashes and squirmed and looked up <u>piteously</u>. Hancock would avert his <u>sensitive</u> face to their <u>distress</u>, "Go away, please" (but he kept pushing them under with his gold-headed cane). Sam Adams would rub his palms and chuckle.

stop+question

What question would you like to ask the author?

....

....

stop+question

Johnny woke up and realized that only Revere and Warren were still in the room and they were talking about Hancock and Adams. These two gentlemen had left Boston in March. They were representatives at the Provincial Congress at Concord. The British had forbidden the General Court to meet, but the Massachusetts men had merely changed the name of their <u>legislative body</u> and gone on sitting. But did the British know that both these <u>firebrands</u> were staying at the Clarks' out in Lexington?

"It will do no harm to warn them," Revere was saying, getting to his feet. "I'll row over to Charlestown tonight, go to Lexington, and tell

◼ V O C A B U L A R Y ◼
piteously—in a way that aroused sympathy.
sensitive—emotional.
distress—suffering.
legislative body—law-making organization; Congress.
firebrands—people who stir up revolt.

them a sizable force may soon move. They had best hide themselves for the next few days."

stop+clarify

What is Revere going to do?

....

....

stop+clarify

"And get word to Concord. The cannons and stores had best be hidden."

"Of course."

"Tell them we here in Boston have the situation well in hand. The second the troops move—either on foot or into those boats—we will send them warning in time to get the Minute Men into the field. I'd give a good deal to know which way they are going."

"But suppose none of us can get out? Gage knows we'd send word—if we could. He may guard the town so well it will be impossible."

Johnny was still half awake. He yawned and settled back to think of those lobsters. With eyes like men . . . long lashes. . . tears on their lashes . . .

Revere was pulling on his gloves.

" . . . Colonel Conant in Charlestown. I'll tell him to watch the spire of Christ's Church. You can see it well from Charlestown. If the British go out over the Neck, we will show one lantern. If in the boats—two. And come Hell or high water I'll do my best to get out and tell exactly

"Ready" continued

what's acting. But I may get caught on my way over. Another man should also be ready to try to get out through the gates."

They talked of various men and finally pitched upon Billy Dawes. He could <u>impersonate</u> anybody—from a British general to a drunken farmer. This might help him get through the gates.

As Paul Revere with Johnny at his heels left Warren's, a man emerged from the darkness, laid a hand on Revere's arm. In the little light Johnny recognized the rolling black eye, poetic <u>negligence</u> of dress. It was Doctor Church.

"Paul," he whispered, "what's afoot?"

"Nothing," said Revere <u>shortly</u> and went on walking.

"The British preparing to march?"

"Why don't you ask them?"

The queer man drifted away. Johnny was surprised that Revere would tell Church nothing, for he was in the very inner circle. Seemingly Revere himself was surprised by his sudden caution.

"But I can't trust that fellow . . . never have, never will."

VOCABULARY
impersonate—take on the personality of; imitate.
negligence—casualness.
shortly—briefly; rudely.

stop+summarize

What, in one or two sentences, happens in "Ready"?

....

....

....

A. UNDERSTAND CHARACTERS Use this cluster to make notes about 3 of the characters in "Ready."

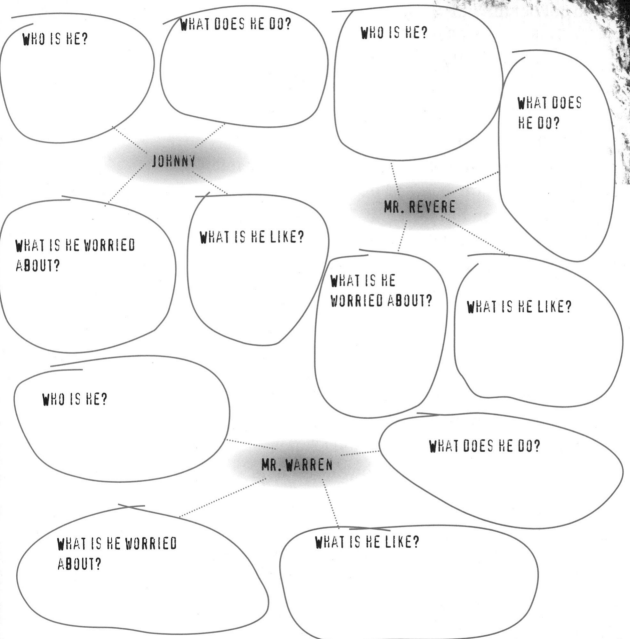

WHO IS HE?

WHAT DOES HE DO?

WHO IS HE?

WHAT DOES HE DO?

JOHNNY

MR. REVERE

WHAT IS HE WORRIED ABOUT?

WHAT IS HE LIKE?

WHAT IS HE WORRIED ABOUT?

WHAT IS HE LIKE?

WHO IS HE?

WHAT DOES HE DO?

MR. WARREN

WHAT IS HE WORRIED ABOUT?

WHAT IS HE LIKE?

B. DEVELOP A TOPIC Choose one character to describe in a character sketch. Brainstorm ideas for your opening sentence by completing the sentence below.

is important to the story because

(character name)

IV. WRITE

Write a **character sketch** of the character you chose.

1. Begin with a topic sentence that introduces the character and tells why he's important to the story. (Check your character cluster for ideas.)

2. Use the Writers' Checklist to help you revise.

_____

_____

_____

_____

_____

_____

_____

_____

_____

_____

_____

_____

_____

_____

_____

WRITERS' CHECKLIST

COMMAS
- ❑ Did you use commas to separate the items in a series of three or more?
  EXAMPLE: The men were ready, able, and nervous.

V. WRAP-UP

What are some of the things that "Ready" made you think about?

READERS' CHECKLIST

DEPTH

- ❑ **Did the reading make you think about things?**
- ❑ **Did it set off thoughts beyond the surface topic?**

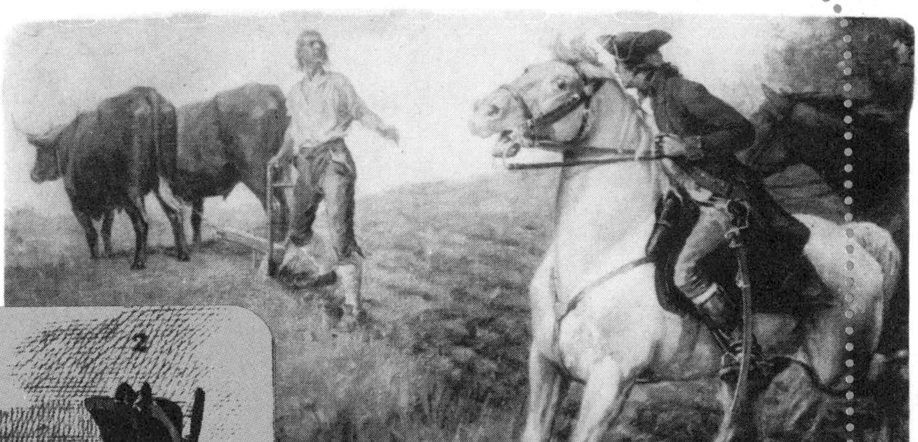

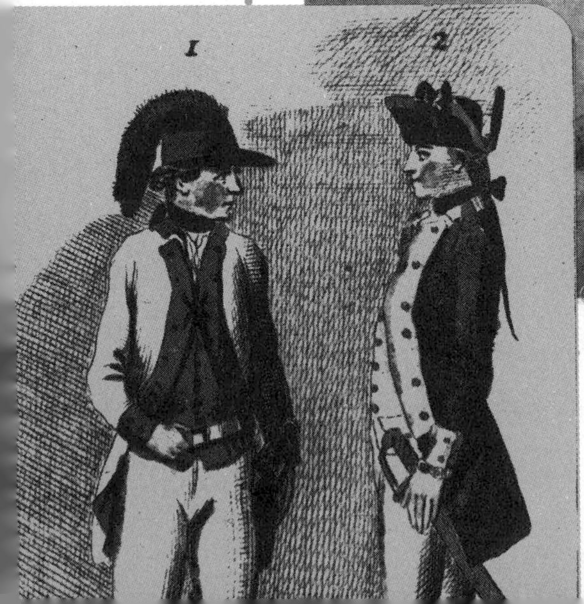

6: It's Tonight

What is your special place? Where is it? What's it like? How does it make you feel? Writers answer these questions when they create settings for their stories.

I. BEFORE YOU READ

Find a reading partner. Have your partner read the story title and first three paragraphs of this second part from *Johnny Tremain*.

1. Listen carefully. Try to visualize what is described.
2. Then complete the Listener's Guide.

Listener's Guide

DIRECTIONS: Answer each question as best you can. If you can't answer a question, leave it blank and come back later.

WHAT PLACE NAMES DO YOU NOTICE?

WHEN DOES THE ACTION TAKE PLACE?

WHO IS WITH JOHNNY?

WHAT DO YOU THINK THE TITLE "IT'S TONIGHT" MEANS?

Listen as your partner or others read the story aloud.
1. Pay special attention to the place names and
   description of locations.
2. Use the Response Notes to note your **reactions** to
   the setting.

Response Notes

"It's Tonight" from *Johnny Tremain*
by Esther Forbes

"It is tonight all right," Johnny said to Doctor
Warren, "and Colonel Smith will command."
He went on to tell what he had found out
from Dove. That the expedition would start
tonight and that Lexington and Concord were
the likely objects, the men sitting about in
Warren's surgery had already guessed. But
they were interested to learn that the Colonel,
and presumably his troops, expected to return
to Boston the day after they set out and that he
was to command them. Seemingly Gage, a
punctilious man, had chosen Francis Smith
because he had been in service longer than
any of the other (and smarter) colonels.

"Hark."

Outside the closed window on Tremont
Street a small group of soldiers were marching
stealthily toward the Common. These were the
first they heard. But soon another group
marched past, then another. A man whose duty
it was to watch the British boats at the foot of
the Common came in to say he had actually

EXAMPLE:
The atmosphere
in the room must
have been
tense.

VOCABULARY
expedition—journey.
punctilious—detailed; attentive.
stealthily—cautiously; secretly.

"It's Tonight" continued

seen the men getting into the boats, heading for Cambridge.

Doctor Warren turned to Johnny, "Run to Ann Street. Bid Billy Dawes come to me here, ready to ride. Then go to North Square. I've got to talk to Paul Revere before he starts. Both he and Dawes will be expecting a messenger."

Billy Dawes was in his kitchen. He was a <u>homely</u>, <u>lanky</u>, young fellow with close-set eyes, and a wide, <u>expressive</u> mouth. He and his wife had dressed him for the part he would play—a drunken farmer. His wife, who looked more like a schoolgirl than a serious <u>matron</u>, could not look at him without going from one giggling fit to another. She laughed even more, and Billy joined her, when Johnny came in and said the time had come. The young man stuck a <u>dilapidated</u> hat with a broken feather on his head and his wife picked up a bottle of rum and poured it over the front of his torn jacket. Then she kissed him and they both laughed. As he stood before them, his expression changed.

His eyes went out of focus. His grin became foolish. He <u>hiccoughed</u> and <u>swayed</u>. He both looked and smelled like a drunken farmer. But he did have money in his pocket which no <u>country blade</u> would have had after a big <u>toot</u>

VOCABULARY
homely—ugly.
lanky—tall and thin.
expressive—showing emotion.
matron—dignified married woman.
dilapidated—shabby.
hiccoughed—hiccupped.
swayed—moved from side to side.
country blade—person from a rural area.
toot—slang word for a wild night on the town filled with heavy drinking.

"It's Tonight" continued

in town. He knew one of the soldiers guarding the Neck that night. He believed he'd get out all right.

stop+organize

Write 3 things that have happened up to this point.

1.

2.

3.

The scene in the Dawes kitchen was so light-hearted and so comical—and Johnny as well as little Mrs. Dawes laughed so hard—he wondered if she had any idea of the risk her husband was running. For by any law of any land a man caught exciting to armed rebellion might be shot. The second the door closed after the young man, Johnny knew. Mrs. Dawes stood where her husband had left her, all laughter wiped from her face. Billy Dawes was not the only gifted actor in his family.

From Ann Street Johnny ran toward North Square. This he found crowded with light infantry and grenadier companies, all in full battle dress. They got in his way and he in theirs. One of the men swore and struck at him with his gun butt. The regulars were getting ugly. He could not get to the Reveres' front door, but by climbing a few fences he reached their

VOCABULARY
infantry—troops who fight on foot.
grenadier companies—special regiments of British soldiers.
gun butt—part of a rifle that rests on the shoulder when a rifle is fired.

"It's Tonight" continued

kitchen door, and knocked softly. Paul Revere was instantly outside in the dark with him.

"Johnny," he whispered, "the *Somerset* has been moved into the mouth of the Charles. Will you run to Copp's Hill and tell me if they have moved in any of the other warships? I think I can row around one, but three or four might make me trouble."

"I'll go look."

"Wait. Then go to Robert Newman—you know, the Christ's Church <u>sexton</u>. He lives with his mother opposite the church."

"I know."

"They have British officers <u>billeted</u> on them. *Don't rap at that door.* Take this stick. Walk by the house slowly, limping, tapping with the stick until the light in an upper window goes out. Then go 'round to the alley behind the house. Tell Newman the lanterns are to be hung now. Two of them. He knows what to do."

As Johnny stood among the graves of lonely Copp's Hill looking across the broad mouth of the Charles, he could see lights in the houses of Charlestown.

VOCABULARY

sexton—person responsible for caring for and maintaining church property.
billeted—living and sleeping there for the time being.

stop+organize

WHAT DID JOHNNY DO AFTER HE LEFT DAWES?	WHAT DID REVERE ASK JOHNNY TO DO FIRST?	WHAT DID REVERE TELL HIM TO DO AFTER THAT?

And over there he knew men were watching Boston, watching Christ's <u>lofty</u> <u>spire</u>—waiting for the signal. And as soon as they saw it, the best and fastest horse in Charlestown would be saddled and made ready for Paul Revere, who had himself promised to get over—if possible. Ride and spread the alarm. Summon the Minute Men. He watched the riding lights on the powerful sixty-four-gun *Somerset*. The British had evidently thought her <u>sufficient</u> to <u>prevent</u> boats crossing the river that night. She was alone.

The moon had risen. The tide was rising. The *Somerset* was <u>winding at her anchor</u>. The night was unearthly sweet. It smelled of land and of the sea, but most of all it smelled of spring.

Salem Street, where the Newmans lived, like North Square, was filled with soldiers. The redcoats were assembling here, getting ready to march down to the Common—and they would be a little late. Their orders were to be ready by moonrise. A sergeant yelled at Johnny as he started to limp past them, but when he explained in a <u>piteous whine</u> that his foot had been squashed by a blow from a soldier's musket and all he wanted was to get home to his mama, an officer said the men were to let "the child" pass. Johnny was sixteen, but he could pull himself together and play at being a little boy still.

▼ VOCABULARY ▼
lofty spire—high, pointed part of the roof on some churches.
sufficient—good enough.
prevent—stop.
winding at her anchor—preparing to move.
piteous whine—cry or sound made in an attempt to get sympathy.

"It's Tonight" continued

Downstairs in the Newman house he could look in and see a group of officers as usual, almost as always, playing at cards. Their jackets were unbuttoned, their faces flushed. They were laughing and drinking. There was on the second floor one light. Johnny couldn't believe anyone up there could hear him tapping in the street below. Instantly the light went out. He had been heard.

Newman, a sad-faced young man, got out at a second-story window in back, ran across a shed roof, and was in the alley waiting for Johnny.

"One or two?" he whispered.

"Two."

That was all. Robert Newman seemed to melt away in the dark. Johnny guessed what the little tinkle was he heard. Newman had the keys to Christ's Church in his hand.

The two friends, Paul Revere and Joseph Warren, were standing in the Doctor's surgery. They were alone. Revere was urging Warren to cross with him that very night to Charlestown. If there was fighting tomorrow, Gage would not hesitate to hang him—at last—for high treason. But Warren said no. He would stay and keep track of the British plans until the very last moment.

"The second a shot has been fired, I'll send a messenger to you," Revere promised.

"I'll wait until then. Why, Revere, I never saw you worry about anything before. I'll be a

VOCABULARY
high treason—betraying the country.

lot safer tonight than you'll be—catching crabs out on that river. Being shot at by the Somerset. And falling off horses—I'll not forget you and Parson Tomley's <u>ambling jade</u>."

He was always <u>ragging</u> Revere about falling off horses. It was some old joke between them which Johnny did not know, and both the men suddenly began to laugh. The mood between them had been heavy when Johnny came in, but now it lightened. They parted as casually as any friends who believe they will meet in a few days. But each knew the other was in deadly <u>peril</u> of his life. It was ten o'clock.

VOCABULARY
ambling jade—slow, useless horse.
ragging—teasing.
peril—danger.

Story Organizer

WHAT IS THE TITLE AND NAME OF THE AUTHOR? ....

WHAT HAPPENS IN THE BEGINNING?

WHAT HAPPENS IN THE MIDDLE?

HOW DO THINGS END?

WHAT IS THE SETTING?

WHO ARE THE MAIN CHARACTERS?

WHAT PROBLEM DO THEY FACE?

GATHER YOUR THOUGHTS

III.

A. BRAINSTORM DETAILS Esther Forbes uses vivid description to paint a picture with words. Get ready to paint your own word picture.

1. First think of a place near where you live that has historical importance.

2. Write that name in the center of the web.

3. Write words that describe the place on the spokes.

What historical significance does it have?

where is it?

place:

What 3 words describe it?

How do you feel about it?

Why is it unusual?

B. SKETCH Now draw the place you just wrote about. Make your sketch as detailed as you can.

IV. WRITE

Write a **descriptive paragraph** telling about the place from your drawing.

1. Use descriptive words from your web. Help your readers visualize the place you are describing.

2. Use the Writers' Checklist to help you revise.

V. WRAP-UP

What did you like most about Esther Forbes's writing? What did you like least?

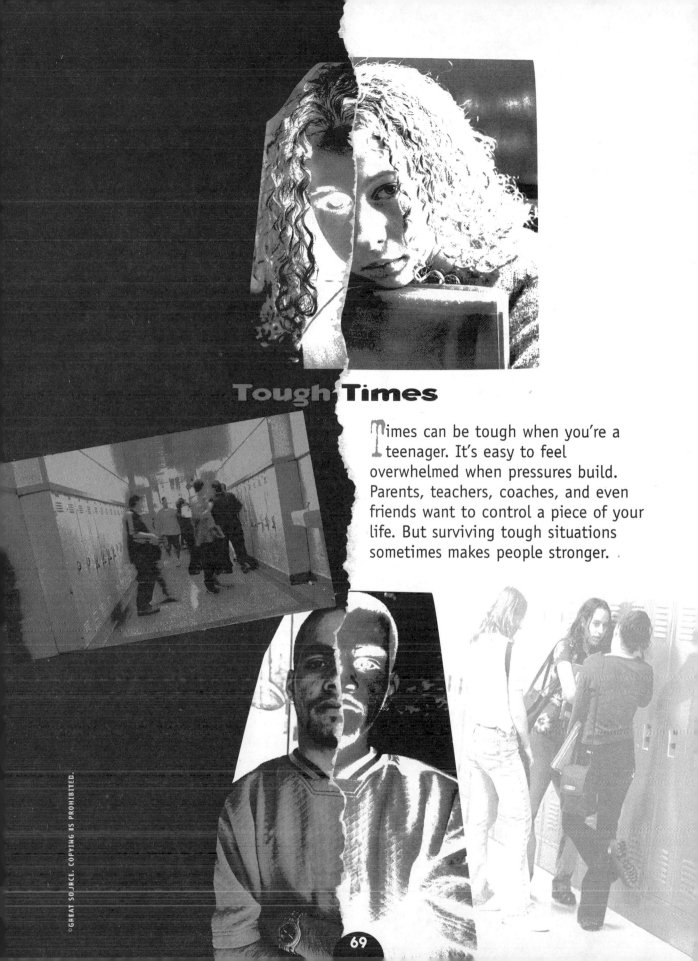

Tough Times

Times can be tough when you're a teenager. It's easy to feel overwhelmed when pressures build. Parents, teachers, coaches, and even friends want to control a piece of your life. But surviving tough situations sometimes makes people stronger.

What do athletes do before they play? They warm up and get ready. Readers need to warm up too. Get into the habit of doing a picture walk before you read. The pictures can familiarize you with the topic and set the mood.

 BEFORE YOU READ

"Walk through" the pictures in this selection.
1. Think about how the images make you feel.
2. Look for clues about the topic of the selection.
3. Make notes on the Picture Walk cards below.

 PICTURE WALK

THE PHOTOGRAPHS MAKE ME FEEL . . .

THEY REMIND ME OF . . .

I HAVE THESE QUESTIONS ABOUT THE PICTURES . . .

I PREDICT THIS STORY WILL BE ABOUT . . .

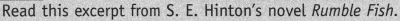

READ

Read this excerpt from S. E. Hinton's novel *Rumble Fish*.
1. **Visualize** the people, places, and events she describes.
2. Make sketches in the Response Notes.

"Hanging Out" from *Rumble Fish* by S. E. Hinton

I was hanging out in Benny's, playing pool, when I heard Biff Wilcox was looking to kill me.

Benny's was the hangout for the junior high kids. The high schoolers used to go there, but when the younger kids moved in, they moved out. Benny was pretty mad about it. Junior high kids don't have as much money to spend. He couldn't do much about it except hate the kids, though. If a place gets marked as a hangout, that's it.

Steve was there, and B. J. Jackson, and Smokey Bennet, and some other guys. I was playing pool with Smokey. I was probably winning, since I was a pretty good pool player. Smokey was <u>hacked off</u> because he already owed me some money. He was glad when Midget came in and said, "Biff is lookin' for you, Rusty-James."

I missed my shot.

"I ain't hidin'." I stood there, leaning on my <u>cue</u>, knowing good and well I wasn't going to be able to finish the game. I can't think about two things at the same time.

"He says he's gonna kill you." Midget was a tall, skinny kid, taller than anybody else our age. That was why we called him Midget.

RESPONSE NOTES

EXAMPLE:

VOCABULARY
hacked off—angry; annoyed.
cue—long stick used in pool.

Read the quotation from the story in the left-hand column. Write how it makes you feel in the right-hand column.

QUOTATION

"If a place gets marked as a hang-out, that's it."

MY THOUGHTS AND FEELINGS

RESPONSE NOTES

"Hanging Out" CONTINUED

"Sayin' ain't doin'," I said.

Smokey was putting his cue away. "Biff is a <u>mean cat</u>, Rusty-James," he told me.

"He ain't so tough. What's he shook about, anyway?"

"Somethin' you said to Anita at school," Midget said.

"Shoot, I didn't say nothin' but the truth."

I told them what I said to Anita. B. J. and Smokey agreed it was the truth. Steve and Midget turned red.

". . . Now why does he have to go and <u>get shook</u> over something' like that?"

I get annoyed when people want to kill me for some stupid little reason. Something big, and I don't mind it so much.

VOCABULARY
mean cat—unkind person.
get shook—get angry.

Use the right-hand column to react and respond to the quote.

QUOTATION

"I get annoyed when people want to kill me for some stupid little reason."

MY THOUGHTS AND FEELINGS

III. GATHER YOUR THOUGHTS

A. REFLECT The narrator in "Hanging Out" faces some trouble. Use the web below to organize your thoughts about the narrator's tough times.

WHERE HE IS

WHO ELSE IS THERE

NARRATOR'S TROUBLE

WHAT THE PROBLEM IS

HOW HE FEELS ABOUT IT

B. DEVELOP DETAILS Now think of some trouble or some tough times you've faced.
1. Begin planning to write a poem about the trouble.
2. Complete the chart below.

The Tough Times:

WHEN THEY WERE	WHO WAS INVOLVED	WHAT THE PROBLEM WAS	HOW YOU FELT

IV. WRITE

Write a **poem** about the tough times you've faced.
1. Refer to the notes from your chart.
2. Use the Writers' Checklist to help you revise.

V. WRAP-UP

What did "Hanging Out" mean to you?

8: Being Fourteen

What's it like to be fourteen? Could there be anything worse—or anything better? If you can make an "instant" connection to what you're reading, you'll find it easier to understand and enjoy.

I. BEFORE YOU READ

Get together with a reading partner.
1. Read these sentences from "Being Fourteen."
2. Put a 1 next to the sentence that you think comes first in the story, a 2 next to the sentence that comes next, and so on.
3. Discuss your answers with your partner. Then answer the question below.

THINK-PAIR-SHARE

"YOU'LL SEE WHAT IT'S LIKE WHEN YOU GET TO NINTH GRADE AND HAVE TO WORRY ABOUT GRADES TO GET INTO COLLEGE."

"THE WORST THING IS THAT THE MORE I REALIZE WHAT I WANT TO DO, THE STRICTER EVERYONE BECOMES."

"IT'S HARD COPING WITH A TEN-YEAR-OLD SISTER WHO WANTS TO BE A STAND-UP COMIC AND TREATS THE FAMILY AS A CAPTIVE AUDIENCE FOR ALL HER ROUTINES."

"IT'S ABSOLUTELY DISGUSTING BEING FOURTEEN. YOU'VE GOT NO RIGHTS WHATSOEVER."

I think this story will be about . . .

_____

_____

II. READ

Now read "Being Fourteen."

1. As you read, think about how the story makes you feel.

2. React and **connect** to particular lines by jotting down your ideas in the Response Notes.

RESPONSE NOTES

"Being Fourteen" from *Can You Sue Your Parents for Malpractice?* by Paula Danziger

"Lauren, why was the skeleton afraid to cross the road?"

I pretend I don't hear Linda.

She keeps talking anyway. "Because he had no guts."

It's hard coping with a ten-year-old sister who wants to be a stand-up comic and treats the family as a <u>captive audience</u> for all her <u>routines</u>. It's especially hard while I'm trying to get over a broken heart.

"Look," I say, "would you please go away? I've got to study my Spanish. There's a quiz tomorrow. I flunked the last one and I've got to get an A on this one, or else."

EXAMPLE:
Funny! My little brother always tells jokes too.

stop and clarify

Who is Linda, and why is Lauren upset with her?

....

....

....

"Just one more. Please, Lauren, then I promise to go."

VOCABULARY

captive audience—group that listens to a performance but cannot get away.
routines—performances.

"Being Fourteen" CONTINUED

I wonder how many other fourteen-year-olds in the world have to deal with a younger sister determined to take her show on the road. It's not that I don't like her, it's just that my mind's on other things right now.

She looks so hurt.

STOP AND PREDICT

Will Lauren let her sister stay in the room or kick her out? Explain.

I say, "Oh, OK. But just one more. I really do have to study. You'll see what it's like when you get to ninth grade and have to worry about grades to get into college."

She grins. "Did you hear the one about the <u>rodent</u> who almost drowned and his brother had to give him mouse to mouse <u>resuscitation</u>?"

"Out," I yell. "Enough is enough."

Linda goes, "Da da di da da da," and tap dances out of the room.

I laugh at the dumb joke after she leaves, and shake my head. She's got a right to her dreams. It's just that my mind's on other things right now.

My special <u>elective</u> class, "Law for Children and Young People," is about to start. And I definitely have lots of questions. It's a good thing the school started it just in time for

RESPONSE NOTES

VOCABULARY
rodent—mammal, such as a mouse, rat, or squirrel.
resuscitation—the act of breathing air into the mouth of someone who has been under water. Usually it is called "mouth to mouth resuscitation."
elective—non-required; freely chosen.

everything I have to ask. The first one's going to be "What are the <u>grounds</u> for <u>justifiable homicide</u>?" Can I kill off one or more of the following: an older sister who gets her own room and ends up with all the beauty genes in the family? A mother who lives in a fantasy world always dreaming about winning the lottery or some big prize so we can all live happily ever after? A mother who's always writing letters and going to tryouts for quiz shows? A father who constantly complains about how hard it is to sell insurance and to support a family in this day and age? Sandy Linwood, who stole my boyfriend because she goes further than I do?

[stop and summarize]

What things is Lauren upset about?

....

....

....

It's absolutely disgusting being fourteen. You've got no rights whatsoever. Your parents get to make all the decisions: Who gets the single bedroom. How much allowance is enough. What time you must come in. Who is a proper friend. What your report card is supposed

VOCABULARY
grounds—reasons.
justifiable homicide—allowing murder.

"Being Fourteen" CONTINUED

to look like. And what your parents don't tell you
to do, the school does: What section you're in.
What's good literature. What courses you have
to take to fulfill their requirements. The worst
thing is that the more I realize what I want to do,
the stricter everyone becomes.

?? STOP aND QuesTiOn ??

In what ways is Lauren like you? Explain.

What do you think is the biggest problem for kids your age?

A. DISCUSS CHARACTERS Get together with others in a small group and review what people wrote in their Response Notes.

1. Compare your feelings to those of Lauren.

2. Answer the questions below on your own and then discuss them as a group.

Which of Lauren's problems are most easily solved? Which ones are more difficult?

What advice do you have for Lauren?

B. LIST Danziger's "Being Fourteen" is sort of like a journal entry.

1. Plan a journal entry of your own about what it's like to be a pre-teen or teenager.

2. Write a brief sentence about 3–4 difficult experiences.

My Experiences

1.

2.

3.

4.

IV. WRITE

Write your **journal entry** about what it's like being a teenager or pre-teen.

1. Describe a single event or experience, concluding with a sentence that ties things together.

2. Then, even though it is just an informal journal entry, use the Writers' Checklist to revise it.

date

WRITERS' CHECKLIST

CAPITALIZATION

❑ **Did you capitalize the names of cities, states, and countries?** EXAMPLES: *Chicago, New Jersey, Japan*

❑ **Did you use capital letters when naming a particular place?** EXAMPLES: *Great Adventure, Deerpath Junior High*

❑ **Did you capitalize the names of specific regions of the country?** EXAMPLES: *the East, the Midwest*

❑ **Did you capitalize the names of specific geographical features?** EXAMPLES: *the Blue Ridge Mountains, the Pacific Ocean, the Chesapeake Bay*

What is the main idea of "Being Fourteen"?

Social Studies

Native Americans

Native Americans have struggled for their rights since the colonizers arrived in America. Troubles began when settlers attacked, robbed, and forced Native Americans off their land in order to make lives for themselves.

Why is it fun to watch a movie preview? A preview gives you a hint of what's to come. It shows you what you have to look forward to and which parts of the movie might be important. A reading preview can do exactly the same thing. It can prepare you for the story ahead.

BEFORE YOU READ

Preview the selection "Attack."

1. Look at the pictures and headings.

2. Then note any character names, vocabulary words, and the questions in the Stop and Think boxes.

3. Make notes on the Preview Card below.

PREVIEW CARD

What clues do the art and headings give you about the story?

Think about the title. What type of "attack" is the author talking about?

What character names did you notice?

Which words stand out?

What does the story seem to be about?

READ

Read "Attack," part of a novel by Ann Turner.
1. **Clarify** key parts of the story as you read.
2. Jot comments about what events interest or surprise you in the Response Notes.

"Attack" from *The Girl Who Chased Away Shadows* by Ann Turner

AN EVIL WIND COMES

When we reach the top of the low <u>mesa</u>, nothing has changed. Yellow aspen leaves flutter in the wind. Sheep's heels click against stones. I love the soft tearing and munching sound of the animals eating dry grass. Kaibah hums to herself and braids a rope out of <u>yucca</u> leaves she's brought with her.

I do not know how long we stay there, watching the sheep. From time to time, I run after our bad goat and swat her on the <u>rump</u> with a knotted rope. She is a <u>mischief-maker</u>, and the sheep always try to follow her. After the second or third time the goat tries to escape, Kaibah calls to me.

She stands at the edge of the mesa, her hair blowing in the wind. She points to the place of the rising sun, where a red cloud smokes up from the earth. What is it? Why does it make me <u>shiver</u>? Trees bend, I try to speak, but my lips are numb. Grabbing a piece of brush, I try to sweep that evil wind away before it can bring harm to us.

VOCABULARY

mesa—flat-topped elevation with one or more cliff-like sides.
yucca—a type of plant.
rump—bottom.
mischief-maker—trouble maker.
shiver—shake or tremble with cold or fear.

RESPONSE NOTES

EXAMPLE:
The heading builds suspense about what is about to happen.

RESPONSE NOTES

Kaibah calls, "What is that cloud, Sister?" But I cannot answer, and I open and shut my mouth silently like a caught fish.

SETTING

Where and when does the story take place?

CHARACTERS

Who is the story about?

OUR DOG IS CRAZY

Kaibah holds her hand out to me. Somehow, I move over the dry ground. The sheep are still grazing, but the dog's <u>ruff</u> is raised as he looks toward the red cloud. When I grab my sister's hand, we look toward home.

"Why are you afraid, Sarah Nita? What's wrong?"

Down below are the two <u>hogans</u> and the small figures of our family, working. Smoke rises from my mother's fire. But beyond the hogans, that red cloud comes closer, closer.

"Is it a storm?" Kaibah asks in a voice so thin, it is like spider silk.

Out of the dust come horses with blue figures on them. Something gleams in the sun, like light on <u>mica</u>. I hear a *pop!* Then another,

VOCABULARY

ruff—fur around the neck of an animal.
hogans—houses made by Navaho Indians of earthen walls supported by wood.
mica—shiny, flaky mineral.

"Attack" continued

then the sound of someone screaming. Oh, let it not be our mother!

Together we race for the path that will take us down to them. But the dog is faster than we are, <u>darting</u> ahead and blocking the narrow way down. Lips pulled back, he snarls at us.

"Silver Coat!" I shout at him. "Get away!" But he does not obey me and stands in front, <u>baring</u> his teeth. Kaibah tries to run past, but he jumps forward and <u>nips</u> her leg. Something pounds inside my body, and I hit Silver Coat with the knotted rope. I have to get down that path! The dog flinches, but does not move, growling so loudly and fiercely that I am afraid he will bite me, too.

That terrible scream comes again, like a *chindi*, a ghost, near a <u>death hogan</u>, and we cover our ears. <u>Huddled</u> together, afraid of the people in blue and afraid of the dog, we don't know where to go. Below, red flames leap from our hogans, and Kaibah groans. Men in blue, mounted on horses, round up our horses and drive them and our family ahead over the land.

Again we try to get to the path, but Silver Coat plants his feet on the earth and will not move. We cannot go forward, we cannot go back. Kaibah opens her mouth and lets out a sound like a ghost crying, and the dog howls with her.

VOCABULARY

darting—running.
baring—showing.
nips—gently bites.
death hogan—dwelling where bodies of the dead are kept.
Huddled—crowded.

What 3 things have happened so far?

1.

2.

3.

SILVER COAT LETS US PASS

How long does it take for evil to come, to break everything you know, like that evil giant of long ago who smashed huge trees and boulders? I wish Monster-Slayer were here, right now, to save us and kill those blue soldiers. But He lived in the Long Ago Time, not now, and we can only stand on the mesa, watching our family become smaller and smaller like birds flying out of sight, until they disappear behind a rise in the land.

Sometime later, when the sun is low in the sky, Silver Coat steps forward and bows to me, waving his tail. Kaibah will not go near him, afraid he has gone crazy. Gently, I hold out a hand to him, and he wags his tail. Then I know; he was protecting us, and now that the soldiers are far away, he does not have to guard us anymore.

PROBLEM

What problem does the character face?

SOLUTION

What does the character hope will happen?

"Attack" continued

Holding our arms across our chests, Sister and I herd the sheep down from the mesa. I think that when terrible things happen, you keep doing everyday things. The sun shines, the leaves blow, and we herd our sheep.

We don't talk, walking slowly at first, then running ahead of the sheep to our hogans. At the edge of camp, we stop, hands <u>clamped</u> to our mouths. There is a bitter, choking smell from the burning hogans; flames and black smoke pour into the sky. Things are scattered all over the ground—mother's metal pot, a sack of food, a bone tool, two sheepskins.

The sheep <u>clatter</u> over the ground as Silver Coat rounds them up, driving them into the <u>corral</u>. Kaibah remembers to run over, close the brushwood gate, and come back to me. Even though I know they are gone, I can't help calling out, "Mother, Father? Aunt and Uncle, Cousins?" as if they could answer from far away. But there are no voices, just the evil crackling of the fire.

I hear a wounded animal sound that makes me turn around to see where it is coming from. It isn't Kaibah, it isn't the dog. It is me.

VOCABULARY
clamped—fastened; covering.
clatter—make noise.
corral—enclosure for confining animals.

CLIMAX
What is the turning point of the story?

RESOLUTION
What happens in the end?

GATHER YOUR THOUGHTS

A. USE A STORYBOARD Use a storyboard to show the main events from the story in the order they happened.

B. PLAN Now get ready to write the opening for a story of your own.

1. Make the story about a time you felt scared.

2. Answer the questions below.

1. What happened?

2. When did it happen?

3. Who was there ?

4. Why were you scared?

5. What happened right before the most exciting part?

Now write the **story beginning.**

1. Start by describing what was happening right before the most exciting part.
2. Describe the characters and setting. Explain who was there and what they were doing.
3. Then finish by telling about the problem the characters will have to solve.
4. Use the Writers' Checklist to help you revise.

What did you think was most interesting or surprising about "Attack"?

READERS' CHECKLIST
ENJOYMENT
- ☐ Did you like the reading?
- ☐ Was the reading experience pleasurable?
- ☐ Would you want to reread the piece or recommend it to someone?

10: On the Red Man's Trail

"What are you trying to do?" When you hear that question, it is probably because someone wants to know your goal or purpose. Readers often ask that question too. Knowing the author's purpose can help you better understand what you are reading.

I. BEFORE YOU READ

Read the Anticipation Guide below.
1. Mark whether you agree or disagree with each statement.
2. Then answer the question below.

DIRECTIONS: Read these statements about Native Americans in the 1800s. Mark statements with which you agree with an "A" and statements with which you disagree with a "D."

	In the 1800s, most Native Americans wanted war rather than peace.
	It was a Native-American chief who first came up with the plan to move all Native Americans to reservations.
	The U.S. government thought the idea of Indian reservations was a good one.
	During the 1800s, white people wanted wars with Native Americans.
	The term *paleface* is meant to be an insult.

What do you expect this selection to be about?

....

....

....

READ

As you read, think about Chief Seattle's purpose in making this speech in 1855.

1. **Mark** or **highlight** phrases or passages that explain the problems Native Americans face.

2. In the Response Notes, write your ideas about what Chief Seattle is saying.

RESPONSE NOTES

EXAMPLE:

Sad fact=
fewer and
fewer Native
Americans

"On the Red Man's Trail" by Chief Seattle

Yonder sky that has wept tears of compassion upon our fathers for centuries untold, and which to us looks eternal, may change. Today it is fair, tomorrow it may be overcast with clouds.

My words are like the stars that never set. What Seattle says the Great Chief at Washington can rely upon with as much certainty as our paleface brothers can rely upon the return of the seasons.

The son of the White Chief says his father sends us greetings of friendship and good will. This is kind of him, for we know he has little need of our friendship in return because his people are many. They are like the grass that covers the vast prairies, while my people are few; they resemble the scattering trees of a storm-swept plain.

The Great—and I presume—good White Chief sends us word that he wants to buy our lands but is willing to allow us to reserve enough to live on comfortably. This indeed

VOCABULARY

compassion—sympathy.
eternal—undying; everlasting.
paleface—white.
vast—great; extensive.

appears generous, for the <u>Red Man</u> no longer has rights that he need respect, and the offer may be wise, also, for we are no longer in need of a great country.

Who is the "Great White Chief"?

STOP AND THINK

STOP AND THINK

STOP AND THINK

There was a time when our people covered the whole land as the waves of a wind-ruffled sea covers its shell-paved floor, but that time has long since passed away with the greatness of tribes now almost forgotten. I will not <u>dwell</u> on nor mourn over our untimely <u>decay</u>, nor <u>reproach</u> my paleface brothers with hastening it, for we, too, may have been somewhat to blame.

Youth is <u>impulsive</u>. When our young men grow angry at some real or imaginary wrong, and <u>disfigure</u> their faces with black paint, their hearts also are disfigured and turn black, and then they are often cruel and <u>relentless</u> and know no bounds, and our old men are unable to <u>restrain</u> them.

Thus it has ever been. Thus it was when the white man first began to push our

VOCABULARY
Red Man—Native American.
dwell—think.
decay—break down.
reproach—blame.
impulsive—motivated to act without first thinking.
disfigure—deform.
relentless—unstopping; persistent.
restrain—control.

<u>forefathers</u> westward. But let us hope that the <u>hostilities</u> between the Red Man and his paleface brother may never return. We would have everything to lose and nothing to gain.

STOP AND THINK

Whom does Chief Seattle blame for the difficulties between white people and Native Americans?

....

....

....

STOP AND THINK

It is true that <u>revenge</u> by young braves is considered gain, even at the cost of their own lives, but old men who stay at home in times of war, and mothers who have sons to lose, know better.

Our good father at Washington—for I presume he is now our father as well as yours, since King George has moved his boundaries farther north—our great and good father, I say, sends us word that if we do as he desires he will protect us.

His brave warriors will be to us a <u>bristling</u> wall of strength, and his great ships of war will fill our harbors so that our ancient enemies far to the northward—the Sinsiams, Hydas and Tsimpsians—will no longer frighten our women and old men. Then will he be our father and we his children.

VOCABULARY
forefathers—ancestors.
hostilities—bad feelings.
revenge—punishment in return for harm done before.
bristling—straight and stiff.

But can that ever be? Your God is not our God! Your God loves your people and hates mine! He folds His strong arms lovingly around the white man and leads him as a father leads his infant son—but He has <u>forsaken</u> His red children, if they are really His. Our God, the Great Spirit, seems, also, to have forsaken us. Your God makes your people <u>wax</u> strong every day—soon they will fill all the land.

STOP AND THINK

What does Chief Seattle mean when he says, "Your God is not our God"?

....

....

My people are <u>ebbing</u> away like a fast-<u>receding</u> tide that will never flow again. The white man's God cannot love His red children or He would protect them. We seem to be orphans who can look nowhere for help.

How, then, can we become brothers? How can your God become our God and renew our <u>prosperity</u> and awaken in us dreams of returning greatness?

Your God seems to us to be <u>partial</u>. He came to the white man. We never saw Him, never heard His voice. He gave the white man laws, but had no word for His red children

VOCABULARY

forsaken—given up on.
wax—become.
ebbing—fading; falling.
receding—disappearing.
prosperity—success.
partial—biased; more fond of one side than another.

whose <u>teeming</u> millions once filled this vast continent as the stars fill the <u>firmament</u>.

No. We are two <u>distinct</u> races, and must ever remain so, with separate <u>origins</u> and separate <u>destinies</u>. There is little in common between us.

To us the ashes of our ancestors are sacred and their final resting place is <u>hallowed</u> ground, while you wander far from the graves of your ancestors and, seemingly, without regret.

Your religion was written on tablets of stone by the iron finger of an angry God, lest you might forget it. The Red Man could never <u>comprehend</u> nor remember it.

Our religion is the traditions of our ancestors—the dreams of our old men, given to them in the solemn hours of night by the Great Spirit, and the visions of our Sachems, and is written in the hearts of our people.

Your dead cease to love you and the land of their <u>nativity</u> as soon as they pass the <u>portals</u> of the tomb—they wander far away beyond the stars, are soon forgotten and never return.

Our dead never forget this beautiful world that gave them being. They still love its winding rivers, its great mountains and its

▪ V O C A B U L A R Y ▪
teeming—many.
firmament—sky.
distinct—different.
origins—beginnings.
destinies—fates; futures that are already set or determined.
hallowed—holy.
comprehend—understand.
nativity—birth.
portals—entrances.

sequestered vales, and they ever yearn in tenderest affection over the lonely-hearted living, and often return to visit, guide and comfort them.

Day and night cannot dwell together. The Red Man has ever fled the approach of the white man, as the changing mist on the mountain side flees before the blazing sun.

However, your proposition seems a just one, and I think that my people will accept it and will retire to the reservation you offer them. Then we will dwell apart in peace, for the words of the Great White Chief seem to be the voice of Nature speaking to my people out of the thick darkness, that is fast gathering around them like a dense fog floating inward from a midnight sea.

STOP AND THINK

How do you know if Chief Seattle will or will not move his people to a reservation?

....

....

It matters little where we pass the remnant of our days. They are not many. The Indian's night promises to be dark. No bright star hovers above his horizon. Sad-voiced winds moan in the distance. Some grim Fate of our

VOCABULARY

sequestered vales—separated valleys.
retire—withdraw; retreat.
reservation—land designated by the government for Native Americans.
remnant—rest; what's left.
hovers—floats.

RESPONSE NOTES

race is on the Red Man's trail, and wherever he goes he will still hear the sure approaching footsteps of his fell destroyer and prepare to <u>stolidly</u> meet his doom, as does the wounded <u>doe</u> that hears the approaching footsteps of the hunter.

VOCABULARY
stolidly—unemotionally.
doe—female deer.

STOP AND THINK STOP AND THINK STOP AND THINK

I think Chief Seattle's goal or purpose was to

ENTERTAIN   TEACH
          PERSUADE   REVEAL AN IMPORTANT TRUTH
          (circle all that apply)

"On the Red Man's Trail" made me feel . . .

....

....

....

Why?

....

....

....

Return to your Anticipation Guide on page 93. Think about how you feel about the statements now. Explain any changes.

....

....

....

....

GATHER YOUR THOUGHTS

A. ORGANIZE INFORMATION List some of the problems Chief Seattle mentions.

1. List problems in the large circles.

2. List details in the smaller circles.

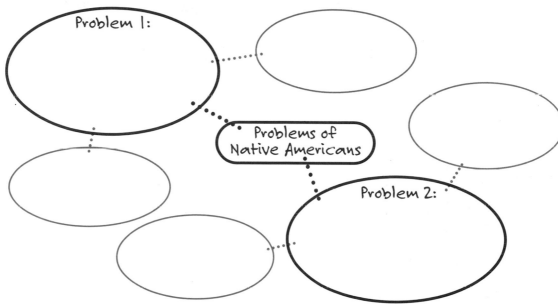

Problem 1:

Problems of Native Americans

Problem 2:

B. PLAN Plan a news article about Chief Seattle's decision to move his people to a reservation.

1. Gather information for the lead, the first paragraph of your article. A newspaper lead tells who, what, where, when, why, and how.

Who? _____

What? _____

Where? _____

When? _____

Why? _____

How? _____

2. Include in your article at least one quote from Chief Seattle about how he feels. Write it below.

Quote _____

_____

IV. WRITE

Write your news article.

1. Start with a lead paragraph and then give some details about Chief Seattle's decision. Include a quotation by him.

2. Use the Writers' Checklist to help you revise.

Chief Seattle Agrees to Reservation Plan

V. WRAP-UP

Did you find "On the Red Man's Trail" easy or difficult to read? Explain why.

Isaac Bashevis Singer

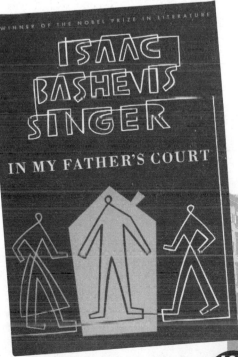

WINNER OF THE NOBEL PRIZE IN LITERATURE

ISAAC BASHEVIS SINGER

IN MY FATHER'S COURT

I saac Bashevis Singer (1904–1991) was born and educated as a Jew in Poland. In 1935, he fled to the United States to escape the Nazis who were invading his homeland. Singer's childhood experiences provided the basis for much of his writing.

Are all people basically the same? Or are they all different? Most of us like to believe that we are one of a kind, each special in our own unique way. "The Washwoman" tells the story of a unique woman.

I. BEFORE YOU READ

Complete the Story Impression below to make a guess about what the selection will be about.

1. Think about what each word means.
2. Then, use each word in the chain in a sentence.
3. Share your sentences with classmates and discuss your ideas about what the selection is about.

Story Impression

MY SENTENCES

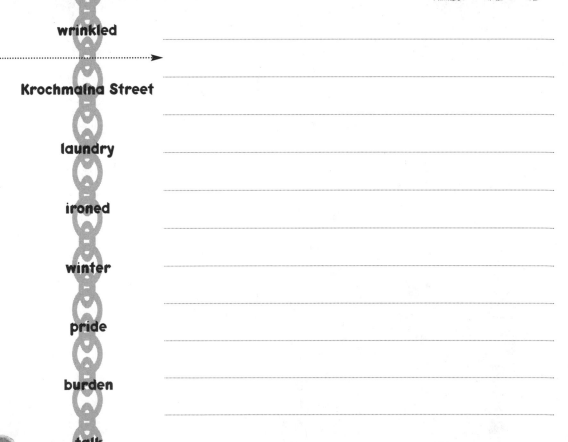

wrinkled

Krochmalna Street

laundry

ironed

winter

pride

burden

talk

READ

Read the first part of the story of "The Washwoman," which is from Isaac Bashevis Singer's autobiography.
1. Watch for information about the main character and think about how you can relate to her.
2. Write your **reactions** to her in the Response Notes.

Response Notes

"The Washwoman" from *In My Father's Court* by Isaac Bashevis Singer

esides the janitor there were also the Gentile washwomen who came to the house to fetch our laundry. My story is about one of these.

EXAMPLE:
I admire how hard she works.

She was a small woman, old and wrinkled. When she started washing for us she was already past seventy. Most Jewish women of her age were sickly, weak, broken in body. All the old women in our street had bent backs and leaned on sticks when they walked. But this washwoman, small and thin as she was, possessed a strength that came from generations of peasant forebears. Mother would count out to her a bundle of laundry that had accumulated over several weeks. She would lift the unwieldy pack, load it on her narrow shoulders, and carry it the long way home. She also lived on Krochmalna Street, but at the other end, near Wola. It must have been a walk of an hour and a half.

She would bring the laundry back about two weeks later. My mother had never been so

VOCABULARY
Gentile—non-Jewish.
peasant—poor.
forebears—ancestors.
accumulated—increased.
unwieldy—hard to carry.
Wola—a city in Poland.

pleased with any other washwoman. Every piece of <u>linen</u> sparkled like polished silver. Every piece was ironed. Yet she charged no more than the others. She was a real find. Mother always had her money ready, because it was too far for the old woman to come a second time.

Laundering was not easy in those days. The old woman had no faucet where she lived but had to bring in the water from a pump. For the linens to come out so clean, they had to be scrubbed thoroughly in a washtub, rinsed with washing soda, soaked, boiled in an enormous pot, <u>starched</u>, ironed. Every piece was handled ten times or more. And the drying! It could not be done outside because thieves would steal the laundry. The wrung-out wash had to be carried up to the attic and hung on clotheslines. In the winter it would become as <u>brittle</u> as glass and almost break when touched. Then there was always a <u>to-do</u> with other housewives and washwomen who wanted the attic for their own use. Only God knew all she had to <u>endure</u> each time she did a wash!

The old woman could have begged at the church door or entered a home for the <u>indigent</u> aged. But there was in her a certain pride and a love of labor with which the Gentiles have been blessed. The old woman did not want to

VOCABULARY

linen—tablecloths, napkins, bed sheets, towels, and the like.
starched—stiffened by adding starch.
brittle—likely to break.
to-do—fuss or argument.
endure—withstand.
indigent—poor.

"The Washwoman" continued

become a <u>burden</u>, and thus she <u>bore</u> her burden.

DIRECTIONS Read the quotation in the left-hand column. Then react to it in the right-hand column.

Double-entry Journal

Quote	My Thoughts
"The old woman did not want to become a burden, and thus she bore her burden."	

My mother spoke a little Polish, and the old woman would talk with her about many things. She was especially fond of me and used to say that I looked like Jesus. She repeated this every time she came, and Mother would frown and whisper to herself, her lips barely moving, "May her words be scattered in the wilderness."

VOCABULARY
burden—trouble; additional responsibility.
bore—carried.

DIRECTIONS In the left-hand column, write 1 quotation from the story that you think is interesting or important. Then respond to it in the right-hand column.

Double-entry Journal

Quote	My Thoughts

GATHER YOUR THOUGHTS

A. COMPARE AND CONTRAST Compare yourself to the washwoman by using a Venn diagram. ⋯⋯⋯⋯⋯⋯⋯

1. Write words that describe the washwoman on the left.
2. Write words describing yourself in the part on the right.
3. Put things you have in common in the middle.

Venn Diagram

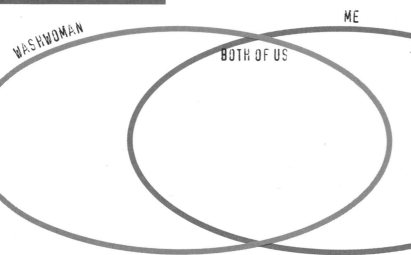

WASHWOMAN

ME

BOTH OF US

B. SUPPORT A TOPIC SENTENCE Prepare to write a compare and contrast paragraph.

1. Use one of these topic sentences for your paragraph (circle one):

> The washwoman and I have a lot in common.
>
> The washwoman and I have very little in common.

2. Then list 3 details that support your topic sentence.

detail #1

detail #2

detail #3

IV. WRITE

Write your **compare and contrast paragraph**.

1. Begin with the topic sentence you circled on page 108.

2. Next write at least 3 details that support that statement. End with a concluding sentence that sums up your opinion.

3. Use the Writers' Checklist to help you revise.

WRITERS' CHECKLIST

CONTRACTIONS

❑ Did you use an apostrophe in every contraction? EXAMPLE: *The washwoman isn't like me because she's so much older than I am.*

❑ Did you put the apostrophe in the right place—where the missing letter(s) would be? EXAMPLE: *I'll (I will) work hard if it's (it is) expected of me.*

 V. WRAP-UP

What did you like most and least about Singer's style of writing?

READERS' CHECKLIST

STYLE

❑ Did you find the passage well written?

❑ Are the sentences well constructed and the words well chosen?

❑ Does the style show you how to be a better writer?

What person do you admire? What do you admire about him or her? What qualities make us admire one person more than another? Isaac Bashevis Singer looks at these questions in the second part of his account of "The Washwoman."

BEFORE YOU READ

Read the statements below.

1. Mark whether you agree or disagree with each one.

Anticipation Guide

BEFORE READING				AFTER READING	
agree	disagree			agree	disagree
⬭	⬭	1. MONEY IS THE KEY TO HAPPINESS.		⬭	⬭
⬭	⬭	2. YOU CANNOT CARE ABOUT A PERSON IF YOU DON'T KNOW HIS OR HER NAME.		⬭	⬭
⬭	⬭	3. SOME PEOPLE ARE MORE DESERVING OF HAPPINESS THAN OTHERS.		⬭	⬭
⬭	⬭	4. DURING TIMES OF GREAT HARDSHIP, YOU SHOULD THINK OF YOUR FAMILY FIRST.		⬭	⬭
⬭	⬭	5. I ADMIRE PEOPLE WHO WORK HARD.		⬭	⬭

2. Discuss your answers with a partner.

3. After reviewing the first part of "The Washwoman" in the last lesson, make a prediction. What will happen in the second part of the story?

....

....

....

....

II. READ

Now read the rest of Singer's tale of the washwoman.
1. As you read, reflect on your view of the washwoman.
2. Write any **questions** in the Response Notes.

"The Washwoman" (continued) from *In My Father's Court* by Isaac Bashevis Singer

The woman had a son who was rich. I no longer remember what sort of business he had. He was ashamed of his mother, the washwoman, and never came to see her. Nor did he ever give her a groschen. The old woman told this without rancor. One day the son was married. It seemed that he had made a good match. The wedding took place in a church. The son had not invited the old mother to his wedding, but she went to the church and waited at the steps to see her son lead the "young lady" to the altar. I do not want to seem a chauvinist, but I believe that no Jewish son would have acted in this manner. But I have no doubt that, had he done this, the mother would have shrieked and wailed and sent the sexton to call him to account. In short, Jews are Jews and Gentiles are Gentiles.

The story of the faithless son left a deep impression upon my mother. She talked about it for weeks and months. It was an affront not only to the old woman but to the entire

EXAMPLE:
Did the woman ever complain about how he treated her?

VOCABULARY
groschen—a small amount of German money.
rancor—bitterness.
chauvinist—someone who is prejudiced or biased.
shrieked—screamed.
wailed—cried.
sexton—employee of the church who cares for and maintains church land.
affront—insult.

<u>institution</u> of motherhood. Mother would argue. "Nu, does it pay to make sacrifices for children? The mother uses up her last strength, and he does not even know the meaning of loyalty."

Story Frame

Who are the main characters in this story?

And she would drop dark hints to the effect that she was not certain of her own children: Who knows what they would someday do? This, however, did not prevent her from dedicating her life to us. If there was any delicacy in the house, she would put it aside for the children and invent all sorts of excuses and reasons why she herself did not want to taste it. She knew charms that went back to ancient times, and she used expressions she had inherited from generations of devoted mothers and grandmothers. If one of the children complained of a pain, she would say, "May I be your <u>ransom</u> and may you outlive my bones!" Or she would say, "May I be the <u>atonement</u> for the least of your fingernails." When we ate she used to say, "Health and <u>marrow</u> in your bones!" The day before the new

VOCABULARY
institution—concept.
ransom—way to make up for your sins.
atonement—amends, as for a sin or fault.
marrow—strength.

"The Washwoman" continued

moon she gave us a kind of candy that was said to prevent <u>parasitic worms</u>. If one of us had something in his eye, Mother would lick the eye clean with her tongue. She also fed us rock candy against coughs, and from time to time she would take us to be blessed against the evil eye. This did not prevent her from studying *The Duties of the Heart*, *The Book of the Covenant*, and other serious philosophic works.

But to return to the washwoman: that winter was a harsh one. The streets were in the grip of a bitter cold. No matter how much we heated our stove, the windows were covered with frostwork and decorated with icicles. The newspapers reported that people were dying of the cold. Coal became dear. The winter had become so <u>severe</u> that parents stopped sending children to the <u>heder</u>, and even the Polish schools were closed.

Story Frame

What is the setting of the story?

On one such day the washwoman, now nearly eighty years old, came to our house. A good deal of laundry had accumulated during

VOCABULARY
parasitic worms—disease-carrying worms.
severe—serious.
heder—private school for teaching students the basics of Judaism.

the past weeks. Mother gave her a pot of tea to warm herself, as well as some bread. The old woman sat on a kitchen chair trembling and shaking, and warmed her hands against the teapot. Her fingers were gnarled from work, and perhaps from arthritis too. Her fingernails were strangely white. These hands spoke of the stubbornness of mankind, of the will to work not only as one's strength permits but beyond the limits of one's power. Mother counted and wrote down the list: men's undershirts, women's vests, long-legged drawers, bloomers, petticoats, shifts, featherbed covers, pillowcases, sheets, and the men's fringed garments. Yes, the Gentile woman washed these holy garments as well.

The bundle was big, bigger than usual. When the woman placed it on her shoulders, it covered her completely. At first she swayed, as though she were about to fall under the load. But an inner obstinacy seemed to call out: No, you may not fall. A donkey may permit himself to fall under his burden, but not a human being, the crown of creation.

It was fearful to watch the old woman staggering out with the enormous pack, out into the frost, where the snow was dry as salt and the air was filled with dusty white whirlwinds, like goblins dancing in the cold. Would the old woman ever reach Wola?

VOCABULARY
gnarled—twisted.
arthritis—painful swelling of the joints.
garments—clothes.
obstinacy—stubbornness.
staggering—moving unsteadily; swaying and tottering.

"**The Washwoman**" continued

She disappeared, and Mother sighed and prayed for her.

Story Frame

What 3 things have happened so far in the story?

Usually the woman brought back the wash after two or, at the most, three weeks. But three weeks passed, then four and five, and nothing was heard of the old woman. We remained without linens. The cold had become even more intense. The telephone wires were now as thick as <u>hawsers</u>. The branches of the trees looked like glass. So much snow had fallen that the streets had become uneven, and on many streets sleds were able to glide down as on the slopes of a hill. Kindhearted people lit fires in the streets for <u>vagrants</u> to warm themselves and roast potatoes over, if they had any to roast.

For us the washwoman's absence was a <u>catastrophe</u>. We needed the laundry. We did not even know the woman's house address. It seemed certain that she had collapsed, died. Mother declared that she had had a <u>premonition</u>, as the old woman left our house

VOCABULARY
hawsers—heavy ropes used to tow ships.
vagrants—homeless people; wanderers.
catastrophe—disaster; big problem.
premonition—bad feeling.

the last time, that we would never see our things again. She found some torn old shirts and washed them, <u>mended</u> them. We mourned, both for the laundry and for the old, <u>toilworn</u> woman who had grown close to us through the years she had served us so faithfully.

Story Frame

What is the conflict, or problem, in this story?

More than two months passed. The frost had <u>subsided</u>, and then a new frost had come, a new wave of cold. One evening, while Mother was sitting near the <u>kerosene lamp</u> mending a shirt, the door opened and a small puff of steam, followed by a gigantic bundle, entered. Under the bundle tottered the old woman, her face as white as a linen sheet. A few wisps of white hair straggled out from beneath her shawl. Mother uttered a half-choked cry. It was as though a <u>corpse</u> had entered the room. I ran toward the old woman and helped her unload her pack. She was even thinner now, more bent. Her face had become more <u>gaunt</u>, and her head shook from side to side as though she were saying no. She could not utter a clear

VOCABULARY

mended—repaired.
toilworn—worn out.
subsided—become less severe.
kerosene lamp—light that burns a thin oil fuel (called kerosene).
corpse—dead person.
gaunt—thin and bony.

word, but mumbled something with her sunken mouth and pale lips.

After the old woman had recovered somewhat, she told us that she had been ill, very ill. Just what her illness was, I cannot remember. She had been so sick that someone had called a doctor, and the doctor had sent for a priest. Someone had informed the son, and he had contributed money for a coffin and for the funeral. But the Almighty had not yet wanted to take this pain-racked soul to Himself. She began to feel better, she became well, and as soon as she was able to stand on her feet once more she <u>resumed</u> her washing. Not just ours, but the wash of several other families too.

"I could not rest easy in my bed because of the wash," the old woman explained. "The wash would not let me die."

Story Frame

How is the problem solved?

"With the help of God you will live to be a hundred and twenty," said my mother, as a <u>benediction</u>.

"God forbid! What good would such a long life be? The work becomes harder and

VOCABULARY
resumed—began again.
benediction—blessing.

harder—my strength is leaving me—I do not want to be a burden on anyone!"

The old woman muttered and <u>crossed herself,</u> and raised her eyes toward heaven. Fortunately there was some money in the house and Mother counted out what she owed. I had a strange feeling: the coins in the old woman's washed-out hands seemed to become as weary and clean and <u>pious</u> as she herself was. She blew on the coins and tied them in a kerchief. Then she left, promising to return in a few weeks for a new load of wash.

But she never came back. The wash she had returned was her last effort on this earth. She had been driven by an <u>indomitable</u> will to return the property to its rightful owners, to fulfill the task she had <u>undertaken</u>.

And now at last the body, which had long been no more than a broken <u>shard</u> supported only by the force of honesty and duty, had fallen. The soul passed into those <u>spheres</u> where all holy souls meet, regardless of the roles they played on this earth, in whatever tongue, of whatever creed. I cannot imagine <u>Eden</u> without this washwoman. I cannot even <u>conceive</u> of a world where there is no <u>recompense</u> for such effort.

V O C A B U L A R Y

crossed herself—made the sign of the cross on her chest.
pious—deeply religious.
indomitable—unbeatable.
undertaken—taken on.
shard—piece.
spheres—places.
Eden—biblical paradise at the beginning of time.
conceive—think; imagine.
recompense—payment or reward.

GATHER YOUR THOUGHTS

A. REFLECT Reflect on the meaning of Singer's story by answering these questions.

1. What was admirable about the washwoman?

2. What does Singer mean by the last lines of the story?

3. What do you think the theme of the story is?

B. PLAN A PARAGRAPH Prepare to write a reflective paragraph about someone you admire.

1. Write a topic sentence that makes an overall point about the person.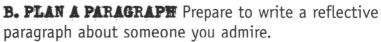

2. Then write 3-4 details that explain why you admire the person.

3. End with a conclusion that sums up how you feel.

MY TOPIC SENTENCE

detail 1	detail 2	detail 3	detail 4

MY CONCLUSION

IV. WRITE

Write a **reflective paragraph** about someone you admire.
1. Begin with your topic sentence.
2. Support your topic sentence with at least 3 details.
3. End with a concluding sentence that explains why you think the person is admirable.
4. Use the Writers' Checklist to revise.

V. WRAP-UP

What are some of the things that "The Washwoman" made you think about?

Decisions

Every day people make choices. They decide what to eat for breakfast and how to spend their money and with whom to spend their time. Making decisions requires a great deal of thought, and we can't always be sure if we'll like the results of them.

Writers are like artists, except they make pictures with words instead of paint. Good readers notice these word pictures. They know the pictures are an important part of understanding and enjoying what they read.

I. BEFORE YOU READ

Get together with a partner or in a small group.

1. Ask someone to read aloud the title and first paragraph on the next page.

2. Listen carefully and try to picture the person being described. Then complete the Listener's Guide.

LISTENER'S GUIDE

DIRECTIONS Answer each question as best as you can. If you don't know an answer, make a guess.

WHERE DOES THE STORY TAKE PLACE?

WHEN DOES IT TAKE PLACE?

WHO IS LOUIE?

WHAT PICTURE DO YOU GET OF LOUIE? WHAT DO YOU IMAGINE HE LOOKS LIKE?

WHAT DO YOU PREDICT WILL HAPPEN IN THIS STORY?

READ

Take turns reading aloud "Louie Hirshfield."

1. Visualize the characters and events of the story, especially Louie himself.

2. Draw sketches of what you "see" in the Response Notes.

"Louie Hirshfield" from *The Zodiacs* by Jay Neugeboren

When I was in the seventh grade at P.S. 92 in Brooklyn, Louie Hirshfield was the only one of my friends who wasn't a good ballplayer. Which is <u>putting it mildly</u>. Louie was probably the worst athlete in the history of our school. He was also the smartest kid in our class and you'd think this combination would have made him the most unpopular guy in the world. It didn't. He wasn't especially well liked, but nobody <u>resented</u> him. Maybe it was because he let you copy from his homework—or maybe it was just because he didn't <u>put on any airs</u> about being so smart. In fact, Louie didn't put on airs about anything. He was one of the quietest kids I've ever met.

The only time I ever saw him excited— outside of what happened with him and our baseball team—was when our fathers would take the two of us to baseball games at <u>Ebbets Field.</u> Louie lived one floor under me, in my apartment building on Lenox Road, and we had grown up together, so I knew lots about Louie that nobody in school knew. He was an

EXAMPLE:

VOCABULARY

putting it mildly—an understatement; saying half as much as might be said.
resented—felt strongly against.
put on any airs—act arrogantly or brag.
Ebbets Field—stadium in Brooklyn, New York, where the Brooklyn Dodgers played.

interesting guy, with lots of hobbies—tropical fish, rocks, stamps, Chinese puzzles, magic tricks, autographs.

That was the one thing the guys in school did know about. I don't know how many days he'd waited outside of Ebbets Field to get them, all I know is he had the best collection of baseball players' signatures of any guy in school. Lots of them were addressed personally, to—like, "To Louie, with best wishes from Jackie Robinson." What amazed me most about Louie, though, was that he could figure out a player's batting average in his head! If a guy got a hit his first time up in a game, Louie would say, "That raises his average to .326—," or whatever it was, and sure enough, the next time the guy came up when the announcer would give the average, Louie would be right.

Louie had no illusions about his athletic ability either; he was never one of those guys who hang around when you're choosing up sides for a punchball or stickball game so that you *have* to pick him. And whenever he did play—like in gym class at school—he did what you told him and tried to stay out of the way.

That was why I was so surprised when he came up to my house one night after supper and asked if he could be on my baseball team.

VOCABULARY
Jackie Robinson—famous baseball player.
illusions—false ideas.

Why do you think Louie wants to be on the team?

....

....

....

"Gee Louie," I said, "we got more than nine guys already—anyway we're not even an official team or anything. We'll be lucky if we get to play more than five or six games all year."

"I don't really want to play," said Louie. "I—I just want to be on your team—"

"Well, I suppose you can come to practices and games," I said, "but I can't promise you'll ever get in a game."

"Honest, Howie—I know all the guys on your team are better than me. I wasn't even thinking of playing. What I'd like to do is be your general manager—"

His eyes really lit up when he said that. I looked at him, <u>puzzled</u>.

"Look," he said. "What do you think makes the Dodgers draw almost as many fans as the Yankees? What was it that made people stick with the Dodgers when they were hardly in the league?"

"I don't know," I said. "They were just Dodger fans, I guess."

"Sure—that's it. Don't you see? Being a Dodger fan means something because being a Dodger means something colorful to the fans. And you know why? Because the Dodgers

VOCABULARY
puzzled—confused.

125

RESPONSE NOTES

have what my dad calls 'a good press'—they know how to get headlines in the papers whether they're winning or losing."

"I guess so," I said. "But what's that got to do with us?"

"What's your team like now? I'll tell you. It's the same as ten thousand other teams of guys our age all over Brooklyn. Nobody cares if you win or lose—except maybe you guys. If I'm general manager, Howie, I'll promise you this—your team will be noticed. Guys won't say, 'We got a game with Howie's team'—they won't come to the Parade Grounds to see all the older guys play. They'll come to see the Zodiacs—!"

"The who—?"

Louie stopped for a second, and I realized that I'd never heard him speak so fast before.

STOP AND PREDICT

Will Howie agree to let Louie be manager? Why or why not?

....

....

....

STOP AND PREDICT

"That's—that's the first thing you have to do, it seems to me." He spoke more hesitantly now, the way he usually did, not looking right at you. "You have to have a name that's different."

"What's wrong with calling ourselves the Sharks?"

"Nothing's wrong with it—but don't you see, nothing's right with it, either. I'll bet there are a hundred teams in Brooklyn alone called the Sharks. Sharks, Tigers, Lions, Phantoms—every team has a name like that. But calling ourselves—I mean, your team—the Zodiacs, will make them different—"

"Sure—but giving us a crazy name isn't going to win us any games."

"Right. What will win you games? I'll tell you—a good pitcher. I've been going down to the Parade Grounds to watch games, making a study of the teams there, and I've found that pitching is about *ninety* percent of winning. Especially at our age, when we're not built up yet.

STOP AND PREDICT

Why might Howie agree to call the team the Zodiacs?

Did you know, for example, that on high school teams pitchers average about eleven strikeouts a game? It's like with baseball teams in spring training—the pitchers are way ahead of the hitters because the hitters' <u>reflexes</u> aren't developed yet."

VOCABULARY
reflexes—abilities to respond and react.

RESPONSE NOTES

"Izzie's a pretty good pitcher," I said. Izzie was my best friend and the pitcher for our team.

STOP AND PREDICT

Who will Louie suggest as the pitcher?

....

....

....

STOP AND PREDICT

"Sure, but let's face it, he's not a <u>top-drawer</u> pitcher. He's just not big enough to be. He's got good control, I'll admit that—but his fastball is almost a <u>change-up</u>. If you let me be general manager, Howie, I'll get the best pitcher in our school to play for us—"

"Who's that?"

"George Santini."

I gulped. *"Him?"*

"That's right."

VOCABULARY

top-drawer—first-rate; very talented.
change-up—kind of pitch in baseball that looks fast but is really slow. It is used to trick batters.

Now return to your Listener's Guide on page 122. Add to or revise your answers.

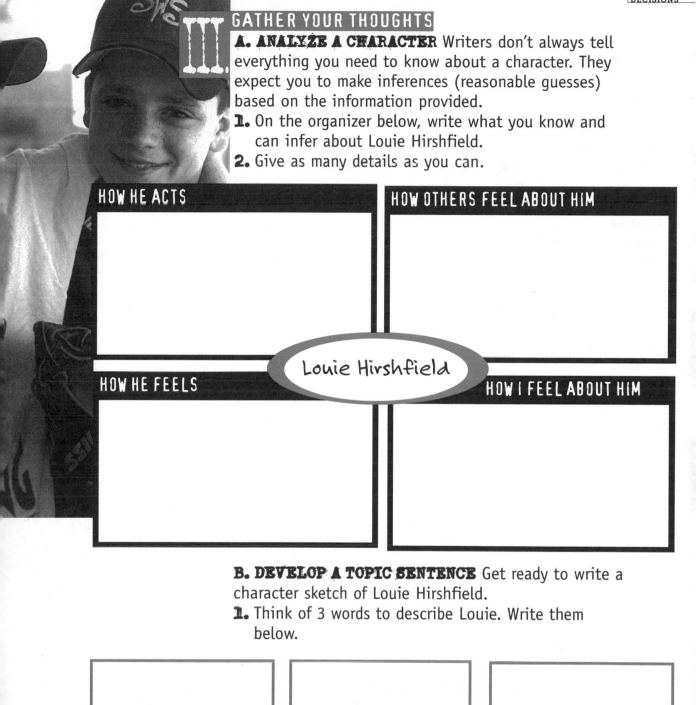

III. GATHER YOUR THOUGHTS

A. ANALYZE A CHARACTER Writers don't always tell everything you need to know about a character. They expect you to make inferences (reasonable guesses) based on the information provided.

1. On the organizer below, write what you know and can infer about Louie Hirshfield.

2. Give as many details as you can.

HOW HE ACTS

HOW OTHERS FEEL ABOUT HIM

Louie Hirshfield

HOW HE FEELS

HOW I FEEL ABOUT HIM

B. DEVELOP A TOPIC SENTENCE Get ready to write a character sketch of Louie Hirshfield.

1. Think of 3 words to describe Louie. Write them below.

2. Then write a topic sentence by filling in the blanks with the 3 descriptive words.

MY TOPIC SENTENCE:

Louie Hirshfield is _____ ,

_____ , and _____ .

IV. WRITE

Write a **character sketch** of Louie Hirshfield.

1. Start with your topic sentence.

2. Then use the notes in your organizer to give details about him.

3. Refer to the Writers' Checklist before you revise.

Louie Hirshfield is

V. WRAP-UP

What was "Louie Hirshfield" all about?

14: George Santini

Have you heard of the saying, "Look before you leap"? It means to take the time to look ahead before blindly jumping into something—and it's good advice for readers.

BEFORE YOU READ

Thumb through "Louie Hirshfield" on pages 123–128.
1. Then preview "George Santini" by glancing through it quickly.
2. Look at character names, pictures, and vocabulary definitions.
3. Fill in the Preview Card below.

PREVIEW CARD

WHO ARE THE CHARACTERS IN "GEORGE SANTINI"?

WHAT DO THE PICTURES REMIND YOU OF?

WHAT ARE SOME KEY VOCABULARY WORDS?

What do you think this story will be about?

II. READ

Now read "George Santini," the second part of Jay
Neugeboren's story in *The Zodiacs*.

1. As you read, think about what you like or dislike
about the story.

2. Write in the Response Notes your **reactions** to the
story's plot, characters, setting, and theme.

RESPONSE NOTES

EXAMPLE:
Funny—makes
me like the
characters.

"George Santini" from *The Zodiacs*
by Jay Neugeboren

George Santini was a year ahead of us at
P.S. 92 and he was always getting in
trouble with the teachers and the cops. He
was about six feet tall, had black greasy hair
which was long and cut square in back, and
the biggest pair of shoulders I've ever seen on
a guy. He was also the best athlete in our
school. The coaches and teachers were always
talking to him about going straight and being
a star in high school and college. But George
never seemed to care much. He was the leader
of this gang, which as far as everybody in our
section of Brooklyn was concerned, was the
most dangerous gang the world had ever
known.

What made George's reputation even worse
was his older brother, Vinnie. Vinnie was
about nineteen years old and had already
spent two years in jail. He was a skinny guy—
not at all like George—and the word on him
was that he was really chicken. To listen to
George, though, you would have thought that
Vinnie was the toughest guy ever to hit
Brooklyn. Whenever he wanted an audience,
George would sit down on the steps of the

school—on Rogers Avenue—and start telling tales of all the jobs he and Vinnie had pulled off. Sometimes, if we'd pester him enough, he'd tell us about the gang wars he had fought in with Vinnie—in Prospect Park, in Red Hook, in Bay Ridge. If he was sure no teachers or cops were around, he'd show us his zip gun, the gun that Johnny Angelo—one of George's lackeys—claimed George had once used to kill a guy with.

STOP AND THINK

Who is George Santini, and what is he like?

....

....

....

"I don't know," I said. "If my mother ever caught me hanging around with him, I'd really get it—and anyway, how would you ever get him to play for us?"

Louie smiled. "You leave that to me."

A few days later I got all the guys together at my house, and I let Louie speak to them. He told them what he'd told me about how he would make our team special, maybe famous—and he also told them that George Santini had agreed to pitch for us. A few of the guys reacted the way I did to this news: they were scared. But when Louie insisted he'd be able to handle George, Izzie and I were ready to back him up.

VOCABULARY

pester—bother.
lackeys—followers.

RESPONSE NOTES

"I say it's worth a try," said Izzie. "Even though I'm pitcher and he'll take my place. I'll bet we could beat lots of high school teams with him pitching for us—"

"Sure," I said. "You ever see the way he can blaze a ball in?"

A few more guys followed our lead, and after a while we all agreed that we'd probably be invincible with George Santini pitching for us.

"One thing, though," asked Kenny Murphy, our second baseman. "How'd you get him to play for us?"

"Simple," said Louie. "I offered him the one thing he couldn't refuse—fame. I told him I'd get his name in the newspapers—"

"Really?"

"Sure," said Louie. "It's not hard. All you have to do is telephone in the box score to the *Brooklyn Eagle* and they'll print it. My father knows the managing editor there. We go to the beach with him sometimes."

For the next few weeks Louie was the busiest guy in the world—calling up guys at other schools, arranging games, getting permits from the Park Department, talking to George and keeping him happy, coming to our practices . . . When he started giving us suggestions on things, nobody objected either. He may have been a <u>lousy</u> ballplayer, but I'll say this for him—he knew more about the game than any of us. Izzie and I gave up playing basketball in the school yard

VOCABULARY
lousy—bad, poor, not very good.

afternoons and weekends and spent all our time practicing with the Zodiacs.

Our first game was scheduled for a Saturday morning, the second week in April. Louie had gotten us a permit to use one of the diamonds at the Parade Grounds, next to Prospect Park, from nine to twelve in the morning, and we were supposed to play this team of eighth-graders from P.S. 246. I was at the field with Izzie by 8:30, but the other team didn't get there until after nine.

STOP AND THINK

What is the setting for the story?

....

....

....

We ran through infield practice and then let them have the field for a while. Kenny Murphy's father, who had played for the Bushwicks when they were a semi-pro team, had agreed to umpire the game. By a quarter to ten neither Louie nor George had shown up and the other team was hollering that we were afraid to play them.

Since George had never come to any practices, some of us were a little worried, but at about five to ten, he showed up. He was wearing a baseball hat like the rest of us, with a Z sewn on the front, and he looked a little

VOCABULARY
diamonds—baseball fields.
umpire—rule on the plays of.
hollering—shouting.

embarrassed. He was smoking and he didn't say much to anybody. Just asked who the catcher was, and started warming up. He wore a T-shirt, with the sleeves cut off. Looking at him, you would have thought he was too muscle-bound to be a pitcher, but when he reared back and kicked his left foot high in the air, then whipped his arm around, he was the most graceful, coordinated guy I'd ever seen. As smooth as Warren Spahn, only righty, with this natural straight overhand motion that every coach spends his nights dreaming about. Stan Reiss, our catcher, had to put an extra sponge in his mitt, but he was so proud, catching George with all the guys looking at the two of them, that I think he would have let the ball burn a hole in his hand before he would have given up his position.

"C'mon," said George, after a dozen or so warm-ups, "let's get the game going."

"We were waiting for Louie," I said. "He should be here any minute."

"Okay," said George. "But he better hurry. I

STOP AND THINK

How would you describe George Santini?

got better things to do than spend all day strikin' out a bunch of idiots."

VOCABULARY
Warren Spahn—Hall of Fame baseball pitcher who was left-handed.
righty—right-handed.

He said the last thing loudly, for the benefit of the other team. Then he turned and spit in their direction, daring one of them to contradict him. None of them did.

A minute later I saw Louie. He was getting out of his mother's car, on Caton Avenue, and he was carrying this tremendous thing. From my position at shortstop I couldn't make it out, but as he came nearer, running awkwardly, holding it in front of him like a package of groceries, I realized what it was: his old Victrola.

"Hey, George!" Louie called. "You ready to break Feller's strikeout record?"

George laughed. "Anytime they get in the batter's box—"

"Wait a second," said Louie. He put the Victrola down next to the backstop. He started fiddling with it, cranking it up the way you had to get it to work, and then he started playing a record. At first it wasn't cranked up enough and you couldn't tell what kind of music it was. But then Louie cranked some more—and I whipped off my hat and stood at attention as the strains of "The Star-Spangled Banner" came blasting across the infield. I looked at George and he was smiling as broadly as he could, holding his cap across his heart, standing rigid, at attention. The team from P.S. 246 must have been as shocked

VOCABULARY
contradict—say that a statement is not true; deny.
Victrola—record player.
fiddling—toying.
rigid—straight.

as we were, but by the time the music got to "and the rockets' red glare—" both teams were standing at attention, <u>saluting</u>, listening, while Louie kept cranking away so that the music wouldn't slow down. People sitting on benches, guys playing on other diamonds, men and women walking along Caton Avenue, a few park cops—they all stopped and started drifting toward our diamond. When the record was over, Louie—in the loudest voice I'd ever heard—shouted, "Play Ball!" and we started the game. We must have had a crowd of over fifty people watching us play our first game, and I'll bet if George had been pitching for a major league team that day he would've pitched at least a shutout.

He struck out all but two of their men—one guy hit a grounder to me at shortstop, and another fouled out to Corky Williams at first base. He also hit four home runs. I got a double and two singles, I remember. We won 19-0, and the next day, as Louie had promised, our box score was in the *Brooklyn Eagle*.

VOCABULARY
saluting—greeting by raising the hand to the cap.

STOP AND THINK STOP AND THINK STOP AND THINK

How is the problem resolved?

GATHER YOUR THOUGHTS

A. EVALUATE Use these scales to rate "George Santini."
1. Be prepared to show your ratings to classmates.
2. Discuss the reasons for your ratings.

THE PLOT IS . . .

| 1 | 2 | 3 | 4 | 5 | 6 | 7 | 8 | 9 | 10 |

not at all
interesting

sort of
interesting

very
interesting

THE CHARACTERS ARE . . .

| 1 | 2 | 3 | 4 | 5 | 6 | 7 | 8 | 9 | 10 |

not easy to
relate to

somewhat easy
to relate to

easy to
relate to

THE SETTING IS . . .

| 1 | 2 | 3 | 4 | 5 | 6 | 7 | 8 | 9 | 10 |

not easy to
understand

sort of easy
to understand

easy to
understand

THE THEME IS . . .

| 1 | 2 | 3 | 4 | 5 | 6 | 7 | 8 | 9 | 10 |

not at all
well-developed

fairly
well-developed

well-
developed

B. DEVELOP AND OPINION Get ready to write a review of "George Santini." Will you give the story a "thumbs-up" or a "thumbs-down"?
1. Select 1 of the 4 story elements to write about—plot, characters, setting, or theme.
2. Then state an opinion about it and give 2 reasons.

The _____ of "George Santini"
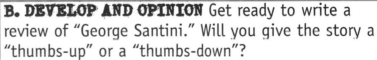
is/are _____ .

Reason #1 _____

Reason #2 _____

IV

WRITE

Now write a **review** of "George Santini."
1. Begin with a topic sentence. Make it clear how you feel about one element of the story.
2. Then give 2 reasons to support your opinion.
3. Use the Writers' Checklist to help you revise.

V. WRAP-UP

What did you like most about "George Santini"?

Child Labor

Child labor continues to be a serious problem around the world. Children slave away in fields, factories, and mines, earning little money and risking their lives each day. Farms have often depended on the labor of children during harvest time.

Have you ever picked up a magazine and paged through it, looking at the pictures? A story's art and photos can provide important clues about its meaning. They can also prepare you for what to expect.

I. Do a picture walk through "You Can't Swallow Me Up."
1. Look carefully at each picture and read any captions.
2. Then complete the sentences below.

Picture Walk

The picture that I spent the most time looking at is about:

I have these questions about the pictures:

I predict this selection will be about:

who?

what?

where?

when?

II. READ

Now read this selection from Tomás Rivera's novel.
1. **Mark** or **highlight** any lines that catch your interest.
2. **Pay special attention to details about what the characters' lives were like.**

"You Can't Swallow Me Up" from . . . *And the Earth Did Not Devour Him* by Tomás Rivera

That day started out cloudy and he could feel the morning coolness brushing his eyelashes as he and his brothers and sisters began the day's labor. Their mother had to stay home to care for her husband. Thus, he felt responsible for hurrying on his brothers and sisters. During the morning, at least for the first few hours, they <u>endured</u> the heat but by <u>ten-thirty the sun had suddenly cleared the skies and pressed down against the world.</u> They began working more slowly because of the weakness, dizziness and <u>suffocation</u> they felt when they worked too fast. Then they had to wipe the sweat from their eyes every little while because their <u>vision</u> would get blurred.

"If you start blacking out, stop working, you hear me? Or go a little slower. When we reach the edge we'll rest a bit to get our strength back. It's gonna be hot today. If only it'd stay just a bit cloudy like this morning, then nobody would complain. But no, once the sun <u>bears</u> down like this not even one little cloud dares to

EXAMPLE:
The heat must have been horrible.

VOCABULARY
endured—withstood.
suffocation—inability to breathe.
vision—ability to see.
bears—beats.

appear out of fear. And the worst of it is we'll finish up here by two and then we have to go over to that other field that's nothing but hills. It's okay at the top of the hill but down in the lower part of the slopes it gets to be real suffocating. There's no breeze there. Hardly any air goes through. Remember?"

"Yeah."

"That's where the hottest part of the day will catch us. Just drink plenty of water every little while. It don't matter if the boss gets mad. Just don't get sick. And if you can't go on, tell me right away, all right? We'll go home. Y'all saw what happened to Dad when he pushed himself too hard. The sun has no <u>mercy</u>, it can eat you alive."

Double-entry Journal

In the right-hand column, write how the quotation makes you feel.

Quote	My Thoughts and Feelings
"If you start blacking out, stop working, you hear me?"	

Just as they had figured, they had moved on to the other field by early afternoon. By three o'clock they were all soaked with sweat. Not one part of their clothing was dry. Every little while they would stop. At times they could barely breathe, then they would black out and

VOCABULARY
mercy—compassion.

"You Can't Swallow Me Up" continued

they would become fearful of getting sunstruck, but they kept on working.

"How do y'all feel?"

"Man, it's so hot! But we've got to keep on. 'Til six, at least. Except this water don't help our thirst any. Sure wish I had a bottle of cool water, real cool, fresh from the well, or a Coke ice-cold."

"Are you crazy? That'd sure make you sunsick right now. Just don't work so fast. Let's see if we can make it until six. What do you think?"

Double-entry Journal

After you read the quotation from the story, write how it makes you feel.

Quote	My Thoughts and Feelings
"Man, it's so hot! But we've got to keep on."	

At four o'clock the youngest became ill. He was only nine years old, but since he was paid the same as a grownup he tried to keep up with the rest. He began vomiting. He sat down, then he laid down. Terrified, the other children ran to where he lay and looked at him. It appeared that he had fainted and when they opened his eyelids they saw his eyes were rolled back. The next youngest child started crying but right away he told him to stop and help him carry his brother home. It seemed he was having cramps all over his little body. He lifted him and carried him by himself and, again, he began asking himself *why*?

"Why Dad and then my little brother? He's only nine years old. Why? He has to work like a mule buried in the earth. Dad, Mom, and my little brother here, what are they guilty of?"

Double-entry Journal

In the right-hand column, write how the quote makes you feel.

Quote	My Thoughts and Feelings
"Why? He has to work like a mule buried in the earth."	

Each step that he took towards the house resounded with the question, *why*? About halfway to the house he began to get furious. Then he started crying out of rage. His little brothers and sisters did not know what to do, and they, too, started crying, but out of fear. Then he started cursing. And without even realizing it, he said what he had been wanting to say for a long time. He cursed God. Upon doing this he felt that fear instilled in him by the years and by his parents. For a second he saw the earth opening up to devour him. Then he felt his footsteps against the earth, compact, more solid than ever. Then his anger swelled up again and he vented it by cursing God. He looked at his brother, he no longer looked sick.

VOCABULARY
resounded—echoed.
cursing—saying bad words.
instilled—implanted; poured.
devour—destroy.
compact—firm.
vented—released; expressed.

"You Can't Swallow Me Up" continued

He didn't know whether his brothers and sisters had understood the <u>graveness</u> of his curse.

That night he did not fall asleep until very late. He felt at peace as never before. He felt as though he had become <u>detached</u> from everything. He no longer worried about his father nor his brother. All that he awaited was the new day, the freshness of the morning. By daybreak his father was doing better. He was on his way to recovery. And his little brother, too; the cramps had almost completely <u>subsided</u>. Frequently he felt a sense of surprise upon recalling what he had done the previous afternoon. He thought of telling his mother, but he decided to keep it secret. All he told her was that the earth did not devour anyone, nor did the sun.

He left for work and encountered a very cool morning. There were clouds in the sky and for the first time he felt capable of doing and undoing anything that he pleased. He looked down at the earth and kicked it hard and said:

"Not yet, you can't swallow me up yet. Someday, yes. But I'll never know it."

VOCABULARY
graveness—seriousness.
detached—removed; separated.
subsided—gone away.

Double-entry Journal

Write your ideas about the quote.

Quote	My Thoughts and Feelings
"Not yet, you can't swallow me up yet. Someday, yes. But I'll never know it."	

A. EXPLORE AN IDEA In his novel, Rivera tells of the injustices a migrant family is forced to endure.

1. Use the web below to explore the meaning of *injustice*.

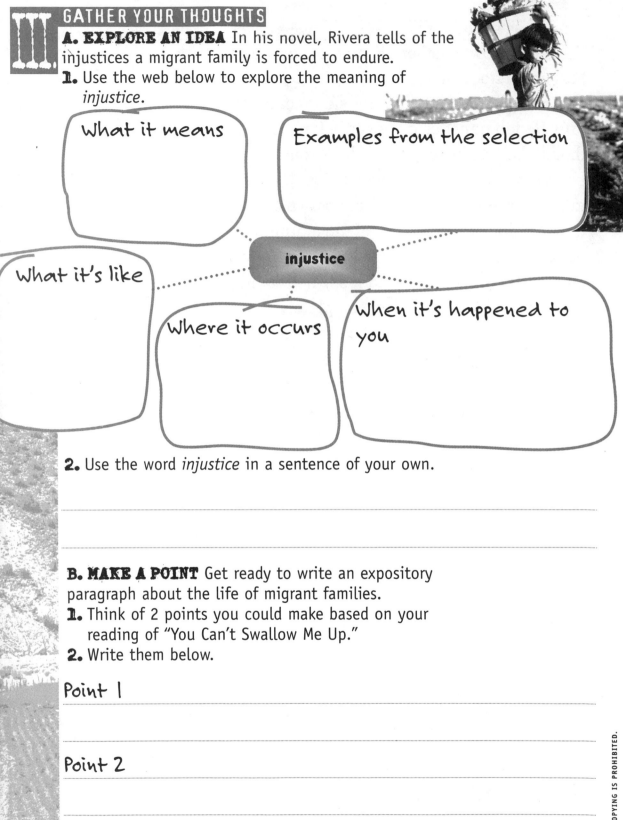

What it means

Examples from the selection

What it's like

injustice

Where it occurs

When it's happened to you

2. Use the word *injustice* in a sentence of your own.

_____

_____

B. MAKE A POINT Get ready to write an expository paragraph about the life of migrant families.

1. Think of 2 points you could make based on your reading of "You Can't Swallow Me Up."

2. Write them below.

Point 1

_____

_____

Point 2

_____

_____

3. Decide which point you would most like to use as the topic sentence of your paragraph. Circle it.

IV. WRITE

Write an **expository paragraph** about the life of migrant families.

1. Remember to start with a topic sentence that states your main point.
2. Support your point with details from the selection.
3. Finish with a concluding statement that restates your main idea.
4. Use the Writers' Checklist to help you revise.

WRITERS' CHECKLIST

USAGE

❑ Did you use *it's* as a contraction for "it is" and *its* as the possessive form of "it"? EXAMPLES: <u>It's</u> a very sad book. <u>Its</u> cover makes me want to cry.

❑ Did you use *their* as a possessive pronoun to indicate ownership, *there* to point out a location, and *they're* as the contraction for "they are"? EXAMPLES: Over <u>there</u> is where <u>they're</u> going to start planting. Tomás is <u>their</u> friend.

V. WRAP-UP

Did you find "You Can't Swallow Me Up" easy or hard to read? Why?

16: Migrant Family Life

Reading can open up worlds you've never seen before. It can also help you look at your own world in a whole new way.

I. BEFORE YOU READ

Get together with a partner. Read the sentences from "Migrant Family Life" below and discuss what you already know about the topic.

1. Put a 1 before the sentence that comes first in the article, a 2 before the sentence that comes next, and so on. Share your answers with your partner.

2. Then answer some questions about the selection.

Think-Pair-Share

_____ "SOMETIMES SOMEONE ASKS ME IF I WAS ENVIOUS OF PEOPLE I SAW IN TOWNS WHO HAD GOOD HOMES AND GOOD CLOTHES AND BIG NEW CARS."

_____ "IF EVERYONE WORKS, THE FAMILY MAY BE JUST A LITTLE LESS POOR."

_____ "WE TRAVELED IN A TRUCK WITH A CANVAS TARPAULIN OVER THE BACK."

_____ "THE KIDS ALL RODE BACK THERE WITH THE BEDDING, FOOD, POTS AND PANS, AND CLOTHES."

_____ "TO BE A MIGRANT IS TO BE POOR."

_____ "WE STARTED PICKING IN THE MORNING AND DIDN'T STOP UNTIL IT WAS DARK."

1. How do you think you'll like this selection?

....

....

2. What do you think you'll learn from reading "Migrant Family Life"?

....

....

Now read this part of Brent Ashabranner's book *Dark Harvest*.

1. As you read, think about what else you'd like to know about the subject.

2. Write any **questions** you have about the selection in the Response Notes.

Response Notes

"Migrant Family Life" by Brent Ashabranner

When I asked Estela about the dark side of <u>migrant</u> life, she talked about the familiar things: the poor pay, the <u>specter</u> of no work, the constant moving from place to place, the <u>bleak</u> housing. "Is there any satisfaction in the migrant life?" I asked.

Estela reflected for a moment. "It is honest work," she replied. "I tell migrant children to be proud of their parents for that."

To be a migrant is to be poor. You may pick three hundred buckets of tomatoes one day and make a hundred dollars, and for the next two days it rains and you make nothing. You stay in the Rio Grande Valley to pick grapefruit during the winter season, but a sudden <u>cold front</u> freezes the fruit on the trees, and there is no work. You are on your way to the raspberry harvest in Michigan when your car breaks down. When you arrive three days late, the jobs are all taken. You finally find work in Minnesota, but the house you thought you could rent for two hundred dollars a month

EXAMPLE:

What do the workers do when the weather is bad?

VOCABULARY
migrant—one who moves around in search of work.
specter—possibility; prospect.
bleak—gloomy.
cold front—cold weather.

stop+think

What are some reasons that migrant families are poor?

....

....

....

stop+think

"Migrant Family Life" continued

Response Notes

costs five hundred. There is always something to keep a migrant poor.

Migrant families that fight their way to a level a little above poverty usually do so at the cost of their children's education and often their health. If everyone works, the family may be just a little less poor.

That is the way it was for Oralia Leal's family. Her name was Oralia Gutierrez then, when she was a child, but everyone called her Lali. The Gutierrez family were migrants in the truest sense. They followed the crops ten or eleven months a year and over the years traveled throughout much of the southwestern and eastern parts of the country. Lali remembers <u>hoeing</u> and picking cotton in Oklahoma, picking cherries in Michigan, bell peppers and cucumbers in North Carolina and Virginia, tomatoes in Pennsylvania, and sacking potatoes in Alabama.

"I started picking cotton when I was ten years old," Lali told us. "I pulled a regular-size sack fourteen feet long, and I could pick as

VOCABULARY
hoeing—digging with a long tool with a metal blade to loosen the soil.

much as almost anyone. We started picking in the morning and didn't stop until it was dark. When we started cleaning cotton in the summer—hoeing weeds—it was so hot you thought you would melt. When we finished picking in the fall, some days it was so cold my fingers were numb. I guess I liked picking peppers best. You could fill a bucket and it wasn't so heavy.

"We traveled in a truck with a <u>canvas tarpaulin</u> over the back. The kids all rode back there with the bedding, food, pots and pans, and clothes. My clothes were always packed in a box. I never had a suitcase.

"If the farm we worked on didn't have housing, we would have to find a place to live. Sometimes it would take a week or two to find a house, and we would just live in the truck. My mother would build a fire and cook our meals beside the truck.

"There was never enough money. Sometimes we didn't get paid nearly as much as my father thought we were going to get. Sometimes we didn't have money for clothes or even food, and my mother would go to the church for help. But she didn't do that unless she really had to. She always bought our clothes at yard sales.

"I went to school a little bit but not much, maybe two months a year. My parents knew it

VOCABULARY
canvas tarpaulin—heavy tent-like covering.

"Migrant Family Life" continued

was important, but the money I could make in the fields when we had a chance to work was more important. I couldn't get much out of school anyway because I didn't speak any English then, just Spanish.

stop+think

Why do many migrant families choose work over school?

"It was a hard life, but there were good things about it, too. The family was always together, and we usually traveled with five or six other families, so we were with people we knew. We were all poor, so we were all the same. And we could still have good times together.

"Sometimes on a Saturday, we would not work or stop work early. We would go to town crowded in the back of a truck, maybe twenty or thirty young men and women, to buy food and clothes and just have a good time. If there was money, my father would give us each a dollar. We would eat ice cream and go to a Western movie.

"Sometimes someone asks me if I was <u>envious</u> of people I saw in towns who had good homes and good clothes and big new cars. No, I wasn't. They belonged to another world, a

VOCABULARY
envious—jealous.

world I didn't know anything about. But there was one thing from that world that I did want. I loved music and I always wanted a record player. I used to look at them in the stores, but, of course, I was never able to buy one."

stop+think

How does Lali feel about her childhood?

Use this chart to show the things that made Lali's childhood bad and good at the same time. Write the difficult parts in the left-hand column, and the good parts in the right-hand column.

Lali's Childhood

What was difficult . . .	What was good . . .

GATHER YOUR THOUGHTS

III.

A. PLAN Get ready to write a 3-paragraph research essay about migrant family life. There are 3 steps to follow when writing a research essay.

STEP 1 Plan
STEP 2 Research
STEP 3 Write

A research planner like this one can help you begin.

Research Planner

my name:

my topic:

due date:

what I already know about the topic:

what I want to find out about the topic:

what I want to focus my essay on:

B. DO RESEARCH You can find some background in "You Can't Swallow Me Up" and "Migrant Family Life." Where else can you find out information?

1. On the organizer below, list 4 places you might look for facts and background about migrant families.

2. Explain what you'd expect to find in each place.

To find out information about migrant families, I'd look in . . .

HERE	HERE	HERE	HERE

WHAT I'D EXPECT TO FIND   WHAT I'D EXPECT TO FIND   WHAT I'D EXPECT TO FIND   WHAT I'D EXPECT TO FIND

C. BEGIN TO WRITE When you've gathered enough information, it's time to get ready to write.

1. Think about what you'll say in each paragraph.

2. Make notes in the boxes below.

PARAGRAPH 1: INTRODUCTION (GET THE READER'S ATTENTION AND STATE YOUR MAIN POINT.)

PARAGRAPH 2: BODY (SUPPORT YOUR POINT WITH SPECIFIC DETAILS FROM YOUR RESEARCH.)

PARAGRAPH 3: CONCLUSION (RESTATE YOUR MAIN POINT.)

IV. WRITE

Now write a **3-paragraph essay.**

1. Use your notes to help you organize the information into paragraphs.

2. Use the Writers' Checklist to help you revise.

Continue your writing on the next page.

WRITERS' CHECKLIST

COMMAS

☐ Did you use commas to set off explanatory phrases? EXAMPLE: Her name was Oralia, or Lali, and she was the child of migrant workers.

☐ Did you use commas to set off introductory phrases? EXAMPLE: In June, we picked strawberries.

☐ Did you use commas to set off interruptions? EXAMPLE: August was, of course, the hottest time to pick.

Continue your writing from the previous page.

_____

_____

_____

_____

_____

_____

_____

_____

WRAP-UP

V.

What did Ashabranner's piece make you think about?

_____

_____

_____

_____

_____

_____

_____

Letters from Rifka

BY KAREN HESSE

Karen Hesse

Karen Hesse knew she wanted to be a writer when she was ten years old. She was inspired by her 5th grade teacher who told her she was "good with words." Since then, Hesse has won numerous awards for her passionate, tender stories like the one in *Letters from Rifka*. In 1998, she won the Newbery Medal for *Out of the Dust*.

Reading and writing go together. Either of them is just fine alone, but they're better when done together. By quickwriting about a subject, for example, you can make a connection between yourself and what you read.

I. BEFORE YOU READ

Read the first paragraph of the story on the next page. Karen Hesse's novel *Letters from Rifka* is about a girl who has to leave Russia in 1919 because she is a Jew.
1. What would make you leave your country?
2. Do a 1-minute quickwrite telling what would have to happen before you would leave your country.

QUICKWRITE

II. READ

Read the rest of the letter.

1. As you read, **visualize** the people, places, and events Rifka describes.

2. Draw sketches of what you "see" in the Response Notes.

"September 3, 1919" from *Letters from Rifka* by Karen Hesse

RESPONSE NOTES

September 3, 1919
Poland

Dear Tovah,

We were fortunate that we ran into no further trouble until we reached the Polish border. At the border, though, guards came aboard.

"Get off the train!" a squat man ordered. His round face and red cheeks did not match the sharpness of his voice.

"Get all your things out of the train! Take off your clothes. A doctor must examine you before you enter Poland."

Can you imagine? Taking off your clothes just like that in the middle of a train yard? Tovah, doctors examine you often because of your crooked back. Is this the way they treat you?

I fought them. I would not take off my clothes for them.

"Do as I say!" the guard barked at me. "Or you will be sent back, all of you."

From the fierceness of his voice I knew he would not <u>hesitate</u> to turn us over to the Russian police.

EXAMPLE:

VOCABULARY

hesitate—wait.

RESPONSE NOTES

I could not have my family returned to Berdichev because of me. I took off my clothes.

I huddled beside Mama as we stood in our underwear in the waning daylight outside the boxcar. Aunt Rachel had made this underwear for me. It was white cotton and very pretty. She had made me two sets, but one was stolen from me as I swam in the Teterev this past summer.

I thought of the things the Russians had taken from my family as I stood in the train yard and I was angry. Why, Tovah? Why is it that if a Russian peasant does not get what he wants, he feels justified in stealing it from a Jew?

stop and retell

What have you learned so far about Rifka and her family?

_____

_____

Papa and the boys undressed on the opposite side of the car. At least they allowed us that much privacy.

Mama and I, we had folded our clothes on top of our bags in the dry grass along the track. The guards picked up our clothes and our belongings and took them away. Even my rucksack with Mama's candlesticks.

Before I could yell to them to bring our things back, the doctor came.

He growled at us. I could not understand his words, but he made it clear what he wanted. He ordered us to remove our underwear.

VOCABULARY

waning—decreasing; slowly ending.
justified—right.
rucksack—backpack.

164

RESPONSE NOTES

This doctor, he stank of vomit and <u>schnapps</u>. His breath choked my throat and I thought I would be sick. Mama did not seem to notice his <u>stench</u>. She smiled and nodded to him. Perhaps she feared he would send us back to Russia. Why else would she act so?

Mama helped me to remove my underwear, shielding my body with her own. Her gold locket hung between her breasts. "Keep quiet for once, Rifka," she whispered in my ear. "Stay behind me."

I covered my nakedness with my hands as best I could, but Mama, she acted as if stripping before the Polish doctor was no trouble, like we did this every day. She pretended this, I think, to protect me.

The doctor examined us. He took longer with Mama.

stop and think

How does Rifka's mother act in front of the doctor?

_____

_____

I could hardly believe this brave woman was the same who wept with fear in your cellar last night. The doctor spent so much time with Mama, he hardly noticed me.

When he did turn his attention to me, the way he looked gave me <u>gooseflesh</u>. Tovah, you are so practical. You will say I had gooseflesh because we stood naked outside in the cold, but it was not the cold that caused me to shiver.

VOCABULARY
schnapps—kind of alcoholic drink.
stench—bad smell.
gooseflesh—goosebumps.

"September 3, 1919" CONTINUED

The doctor made me feel dirty. He looked in my eyes and my mouth and my hair. "Are you sick?" he asked me in Russian.

I kept my eyes down. I could not stand to look at him. I stared instead at my toes curled tight in the stones at the edge of the tracks. I prayed the doctor would just go away.

He yelled at me, something in Polish. Mama spoke with him.

Then she took my hand and led me into a small building. In the building, a woman sprayed us with something <u>vile</u>. It burned my skin and my scalp, my nose and my eyes.

Finally the Polish guards allowed us back onto the train. They returned our clothes to us and our bags, stinking of <u>fumigation</u>. My eyes watered from the stench of it.

stop and think

How does Rifka feel about the doctor's exam?

_____

_____

That was not the worst, though. When I lifted my rucksack, it was not as heavy as it had been before. I searched the entire bag, emptying it out on the floor of the train, but Mama's candlesticks were gone.

"So they stole our candlesticks," Mama said. "It could be worse, Rifka, much worse. Stop sniffling and finish getting dressed."

VOCABULARY

vile—disgusting.
fumigation—smoke and fumes used to disinfect.

RESPONSE NOTES

We pulled our clothes back on before Papa and Nathan and Saul joined us. Mama sighed with relief as they climbed into the car.

I turned away from their nakedness. How could the Poles do this to my papa, to my brothers? How could the Poles do this to me?

The train started moving before Papa and the boys finished dressing. That is how we entered Poland.

I have never been in another country before, not even in another village. You know how the Russians kept us, Tovah, like prisoners, never permitting us to travel. Russia has not been so bad for you. With money, Russia can be very good, even for a Jew. For us it was a prison.

Poland does not look that different from Berdichev. The same crooked cottages, the same patchy roads, the same bony fences leaning into the dust. Looking out from the train, we see people dressed like us, in browns and blacks; people wrapped in layers of clothes. The women bundle their heads in kerchiefs, the men shuffle along in ankle coats and boots. Will it be like this in America too?

I will stop writing for now. My head throbs and my body aches from all that has happened.

> Shalom, my cousin,
> Rifka

VOCABULARY
permitting—letting.
kerchiefs—pieces of cloth worn over the head.
shuffle—move slowly.
Shalom—the Hebrew word for "peace."

III. GATHER YOUR THOUGHTS

A. NARROW THE TOPIC Get ready to write a paragraph about an experience that happened to you or your family.

1. First narrow your topic. Look at the example.

2. Then narrow your own topic the same way.

EXAMPLE

Very broad.
> An important experience that happened to my family

↓

Still too broad. Covers too much time and too many places.
> My sister got sick

↓

> She had surgery

↓

Topic is narrowed to one place, one time.
> How I felt as I waited in the hospital waiting room.

An important experience that happened to my family

↓

↓

↓

B. DEVELOP THE TOPIC Next develop your narrowed topic. Tell about the experience. Put the events in order.

1.

2.

3.

4.

IV. WRITE

Write your own **personal experience** paragraph.

1. Start with a topic sentence. Tell what the experience was and how it affected you.

2. Use the Writers' Checklist to help you revise.

WRITERS' CHECKLIST

CONFUSING PAIRS

❑ Did you use *farther* when referring to a physical distance, and *further* to mean "additional"?

EXAMPLES: *He ran farther. Look for further information.*

❑ Did you use *fewer* to refer to the number of separate units and *less* to refer to bulk quantity?

EXAMPLE: *There is less sand, so we'll make fewer sandcastles.*

V. WRAP-UP

What did you like most about Karen Hesse's style of writing? What did you like least?

READERS' CHECKLIST

STYLE

❑ Did you find the passage well written?

❑ Are the sentences well constructed and the words well chosen?

Do you ever browse in store windows? Perhaps you take quick looks here and there, stopping if you see something that interests you. When you walk through a selection before you read it, you do the same thing.

BEFORE YOU READ

Do a walk-through of "October 5, 1919," another selection from *Letters from Rifka*.

1. Read the several paragraphs on the next page.

2. Then thumb through the rest, looking for dates, times, vocabulary words, and names of people and places.

3. Complete the sentences below.

WALK-THROUGH

WHAT I LEARNED FROM READING THE OPENING PARAGRAPHS:

_____

_____

I NOTICED THESE VOCABULARY WORDS:

_____

I NOTICED THESE . . .

    DATES AND TIMES: _____

    PLACE NAMES: _____

    CHARACTER NAMES: _____

I THINK THE STORY WILL BE ABOUT: _____

_____

I THINK IT WILL BE   EASY   AVERAGE   DIFFICULT   TO READ.

(c i r c l e   o n e)

READ

Read "October 5, 1919" slowly and carefully.

1. As you're reading, **predict** what will happen to Rifka and her family.

2. Write your predictions in the Response Notes.

"October 5, 1919" from *Letters from Rifka*
by Karen Hesse

RESPONSE NOTES

October 5, 1919
Motziv, Poland

Dear Tovah,

I thought we would be in America by now, but we remain in Poland, stranded by illness.

The sickness began with me. My legs and head started aching shortly after we crossed the Polish border.

I told Papa, "I am tired. That spray has made me sick."

By the time we arrived in Motziv my head pounded and my body hurt as if the train had run over me. I wanted only to rest. The motion of the train <u>tormented</u> me. I begged Papa for us to stop.

Mama and Papa took me off the train in Motziv. I did not know Papa had a cousin here, did you, Tovah? Papa's cousin did not have room for us, but he took us in anyway.

I don't remember very well what happened the first few weeks in Motziv. We slept on the floor in the shed of my father's cousin. I had dreams, terrible dreams about the guards at the train station and <u>Cossacks</u> and entire forests chasing after me. Such nightmares!

EXAMPLE:
Rifka will go to a doctor.

VOCABULARY

tormented—upset.

Cossacks—people from the southern part of Russia.

RESPONSE NOTES

I could not move at all. I felt imprisoned under a mound of stones.

I remember Papa down on the floor beside me, putting a damp cloth on my head. Papa is so good at nursing, but each time he placed the cloth over my eyes, I felt the weight of it crushing my head to the floor.

I tried to pull away from him, but whenever I moved, the pain exploded inside me. I begged Papa to stop, but the words would not come out. I could hardly draw breath, there was such a heaviness on my chest.

STOP AND PREDICT

Will Rifka recover or not? Explain how you know.

_____

_____

_____

Saul says a student of medicine came to examine me. Papa had found a student to come who spoke Russian. By then a rash had crept under my armpits and across my back and my stomach. I had a cough that threatened to split me in two each time it <u>erupted</u> from me.

I had <u>typhus</u>.

The medical student said, "Her infection started in Russia. Someone she had contact with there gave this to her."

VOCABULARY
erupted—came out.
typhus—a disease caused by fleas or lice.

172

RESPONSE NOTES

I wanted to tell this skinny, <u>pock-faced</u> man that he was wrong, that my illness did not come from Russia. I knew where it started. It came from the doctor at the Polish border. I tried to explain this to the man, but I could not speak.

"You must say nothing about the nature of her illness to anyone," the medical student told Papa. "Not even to your cousin. As for the child, she will probably die. Most do. That's how it goes with typhus. "

I remember very little, Tovah, but I do remember that. Those words cut through the fever and the pain. When I heard them, I wished I could die. If I died, I would be free of my suffering.

stop and clarify

What does the medical student think is wrong with Rifka?

_____

_____

_____

But if I died, I would never reach America.

I remember Mama crying. I tried to speak, to say I would not die, that nothing would hold me back from America, but she couldn't hear me. No one could hear me.

"I should send you all back to Russia," the medical student said. "But the child would never survive the trip."

VOCABULARY
pock-faced—scar-faced.

Papa begged him to let us stay. "I promise to care for her," he said.

The medical student agreed.

I lapsed into sleep on the floor in the miserable little shed while the typhus raged inside me.

Meanwhile, Mama and Papa and Nathan grew sick. They developed the typhus too. Only Saul managed to stay healthy. Saul is too much of an ox to get sick, Tovah.

Three men took Mama and Papa and Nathan in a cart to a hospital at the other end of Motziv.

I wept to see them go. I was still so sick, but I wept to see them. As they carried Papa out and loaded him into the cart beside Mama, I thought my life was over.

stop and clarify

Why does Rifka feel like her "life was over"?

_____

_____

_____

"Take me too!" I cried, but I had improved compared to Mama and Papa and Nathan.

"Motziv is full of typhus," the cart driver said. "We need the beds for the dying."

They left me with Saul, of all people. Saul, who never has a kind word for me. Saul, who pulls my hair and punches me, even though Mama says at sixteen he should know better.

VOCABULARY
lapsed—fell.

"October 5, 1919" CONTINUED

Saul, with his big ears and his big feet, was all I had for a nurse.

It is a wonder I did not die from the typhus. When Saul remembered, he held water to my lips so I could drink.

In my dreams and when I woke, I <u>fretted</u> over Mama and Papa and Nathan. Were they already dead?

"Where is Mama?" I asked each time I woke from a restless fever sleep. "Where is Papa?"

Saul turned his face away. He could not stand the smell of me; I could tell by the way his mouth tightened. "Go back to sleep, Rifka," he said. He always said the same. "Go back to sleep."

[stop and summarize]

Who is Saul, and why is he taking care of Rifka?

....

....

Once I woke to find Saul kneeling beside me, holding my hands down. His dark hair curled wildly around his ears. "What are you doing to yourself?" he kept asking.

I had been dreaming about Mama's candlesticks. I was holding them against my chest. Hands, dozens of hands, reached out of the darkness to take them from me. I tore at the

VOCABULARY
fretted—worried.

hands, trying to get them off me, trying to get them off Mama's candlesticks.

"Look what you've done to yourself," Saul said, touching the tail of his shirt to my chest.

In my sleep, I had clawed at my chest until it bled.

Tovah, my hand is too weak to continue and my eyes blur at these tiny letters, but I will write again soon.

Shalom,

Rifka

?? STOP aND QuesTiOn ??

What questions do you have about Rifka and her illness?

....

....

....

....

....

III. GATHER YOUR THOUGHTS

A. CONNECT The little stories that writers tell to help make a point or support an argument are called anecdotes. Think of a time you were ill.

1. Write an anecdote that shows how sick you really were.

2. Ask a reading partner to comment on your writing.

MY ANECDOTE

_____

_____

_____

_____

_____

B. BRAINSTORM DETAILS Get ready to write an autobiographical paragraph about a time you felt really sick. Use the organizer below to help you brainstorm details about the experience.

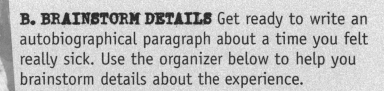

HOW DID YOU FEEL?

WHAT WAS WRONG WITH YOU?

WHEN DID THIS HAPPEN?

WHO TOOK CARE OF YOU?

WHERE WERE YOU?

HOW LONG WERE YOU SICK?

WHAT HELPED YOU RECOVER?

IV. WRITE

Write your **autobiographical paragraph** here.
1. Write in the first person.
2. Start by completing the topic sentence. Use your notes from the previous page to help you.
3. Use the Writers' Checklist to help you revise.

When I was _____ years old, I . . .

WRITERS' CHECKLIST
USAGE

☐ Did you use *to* as a preposition to mean "in the direction of," *too* to mean "also" or "very," and *two* to mean the number?

EXAMPLE: *The two children went to the store too, along with their parents.*

V. WRAP-UP

What did Hesse's writing make you think about?

READERS' CHECKLIST
DEPTH

☐ Did the reading make you think about things?
☐ Did it set off thoughts beyond the surface topic?

Self-reliance

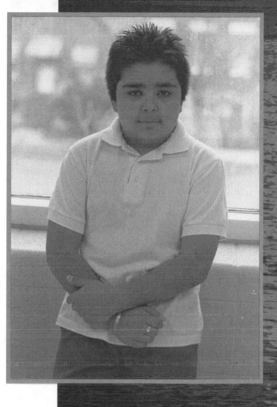

ometimes, the only person
you can count on is yourself.
When friends and family
members aren't around, and
when times get rough, it's up to
you to make the best of the
situation.

Everybody is a little scared sometimes. Maybe you have felt scared about a test or a dance, but have you ever felt really and truly afraid? In "Escape," a young woman becomes afraid after she takes off on a dangerous journey.

BEFORE YOU READ

Complete the Anticipation Guide below.

1. Read each of these statements and mark whether you agree or disagree.
2. Return to the statements later, after you've finished reading "Escape," and mark your answers again.

ANTICIPATION GUIDE

BEFORE READING			AFTER READING	
agree	disagree		agree	disagree
☐	☐	SLEEPING ALONE AT NIGHT IN A JUNGLE IS NO BIG DEAL.	☐	☐
☐	☐	TELLING YOURSELF A STORY CAN CALM YOU DOWN.	☐	☐
☐	☐	AN ANIMAL'S FIRST INSTINCT IS TO PROTECT ITS YOUNG.	☐	☐
☐	☐	YOU CAN'T STARVE TO DEATH IF YOU ARE SURROUNDED BY FISH AND WILDLIFE.	☐	☐
☐	☐	HIPPOS BRING GOOD LUCK.	☐	☐
☐	☐	THE WIND CAN TALK TO YOU.	☐	☐

READ

Now read "Escape," an excerpt from Nancy Farmer's novel.

1. Make notes that help you **clarify** the story's events.
2. Number the key events in the Response Notes.

"Escape" from *A Girl Named Disaster* by Nancy Farmer

She set off before dawn. "I wasted too much time yesterday," she said. In her mind was the possibility that if she tried really hard, she might reach <u>Zimbabwe</u> by dark. She didn't want to spend another night alone. She was terribly stiff from rowing and sleeping in the damp, but as she paddled, the soreness went away. The sun dried her dress-cloth and raised her spirits.

The honey-and-millet cakes were almost gone. Good as they were, at any rate, Nhamo <u>craved</u> variety. In the middle of the day she tied up to an immense <u>strangler fig</u> and <u>clambered</u> over it to reach land. There she set about making a fire. She boiled <u>mealie meal</u> and sprinkled it with dried fish. She had even taken a precious packet of salt for flavoring.

This was living! With her stomach comfortably stretched, she <u>dozed</u> awhile and set out again.

VOCABULARY
Zimbabwe—a country in southeast Africa.
craved—greatly desired.
strangler fig—tree.
clambered—climbed.
mealie meal—corn meal; mush.
dozed—slept lightly.

EXAMPLE:
1. Nhamo leaves by boat for Zimbabwe.

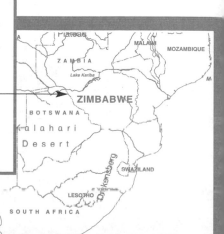

RESPONSE NOTES

In mid-afternoon, a hippo rose out of the water right beside her and opened his huge mouth. He roared—she could see right down his pink gullet—and snapped his teeth at her. Nhamo threw herself flat in the boat. *Aunh-aunh-aunh* went the hippo. A splash told her he had submerged. A second later the boat rocked. He was bumping it!

Nhamo grabbed the oar and began rowing for shore. Other hippos surfaced around her. They kept pace, their piggy eyes just above the water. The male yawned again, terrifyingly. Nhamo had never seen a hippo's mouth so close-up. It looked like a slab of raw meat studded with teeth. *Aunh-aunh-aunh* went the beast, rearing his head toward the sky. He looked as though he wouldn't mind chopping her boat in two!

She saw babies on the outskirts of the group. She knew that few things were more dangerous than hippos with young.

Nhamo paddled. She used muscles she hadn't known she possessed. She prayed to every spirit she could think of, even her great-

VOCABULARY
gullet—throat.
submerged—gone under water.
surfaced—appeared out of the water.
outskirts—edges.

"Escape" continued

grandfather whom she had never seen. The water became shallow—the boat scraped on stone—and she despaired of escaping. But the hippos didn't care for the shallows. They fell back to the deeper water and floated there in a long line.

2. Who are the characters up to this point?

Nhamo jumped out and splashed up to her waist in water. Without her weight, the boat floated free. It began spinning away downstream. She caught it with the tips of her fingers and fought desperately until she was able to plant her feet firmly on the riverbed and pull the craft within reach of a tree.

She sat on shore the rest of the day. The hippos floated near and far. They returned frequently to observe her. It was too unfair! She had been making such good progress. She could almost imagine the electric lights of Zimbabwe, but when darkness fell there was not a shred of light in the forest. She was utterly alone.

The hippos talked among themselves. Finally, silence fell as the huge animals left the water and went <u>foraging</u> for grass. Nhamo

VOCABULARY
foraging—searching for food.

RESPONSE NOTES

climbed back into the boat and <u>resigned</u> herself to another <u>miserable</u> night.

STORY FRAME STORY FRAME 3. What is the conflict or problem of the story?

She didn't sleep well. When the hippos were silent, she imagined them creeping around the tree where she had tied up. Toward dawn, when they returned to the water, their grunts echoed <u>distressingly</u> close by. The red sunlight on the water showed their glistening heads in the deeper channel. They kept sinking and surfacing, but Nhamo thought she could see twenty adults and six babies.

Her bones ached, and her skin itched from the constant damp. Around midday she finished the last of the honey-and-millet cakes. Now she would have to go on shore to cook, but she couldn't bring herself to face the danger. It was easier to lie in the boat and tell herself stories: the many, many stories she had soaked up from Grandmother and from hiding in the darkness near the men's *dare*.

"One day Mwari was thinking about the things he had made," Nhamo told Mother in the jar. "He looked at the sun, the moon, and

VOCABULARY
resigned—gave up; submitted.
miserable—very unhappy.
distressingly—worrisomely.

the stars. He looked at the sky and the clouds. 'I think I'll make something even more beautiful,' he said, so he created Mother Earth.

"He made her in the shape of a <u>winnowing basket</u> and gave her water from the clouds and fire from the sun. He covered her with trees and bushes and grass. 'I give you the power to make these things grow,' he told Mother Earth.

"Mwari spoke so often of his beautiful Earth, the sun and moon became jealous. The sun grew hot and tried to burn her; the moon chased away the clouds to dry her up. But the trees and grass continued to grow. The heat only made them put out more flowers.

"The sun and moon complained so much, Mwari decided he would have to make something to eat the plants. Then Mother Earth would not be quite so beautiful. He took clay and made the animals. He worked quickly because he had a lot of animals to create. He worked so fast he forgot to give horns to some or tails to others. Some animals had big ears, others no ears at all. As the day passed and the sun began to go down, Mwari became tired. He took a big lump of clay, poked holes in it for eyes, and stuck a few <u>bristles</u> on its <u>rump</u>. 'There! I'm too tired to create anything else,' Mwari said.

VOCABULARY

winnowing basket—container made from grasses or reeds used to hold and sift grain.
bristles—stiff hairs.
rump—bottom.

"The last animal was only half made. It was very ugly and bad-tempered. It was the hippopotamus.

"Even Mwari doesn't like you," Nhamo called out over the river. "He makes you hide in the water so he doesn't have to look at you."

The hippopotamuses continued to doze with their noses above the surface.

"The next day, the water complained," Nhamo went on. "'The land is full of creatures. What about me?' Mwari took more clay and made the fishes, only he didn't have much left, so he couldn't give them legs. He told Mother Earth to bring everything to life."

Nhamo looked over the edge of the boat. A big catfish foraged along the bottom. She could roast it over *mopane* coals with a little salt for flavoring. Ah! She could almost taste it now! Her mouth watered. Slowly, <u>stealthily</u>, she slid her hand into the river and wiggled a finger very slowly. The fish drew closer; its fins stroked the <u>sluggish current</u>. It hesitated, watching the finger.

Nhamo <u>lunged</u> with both hands, but the catfish was even faster. It shot out of the shallows and disappeared under a raft of <u>water lettuce</u>. She sat back down with her hands clasped across her grumbling stomach.

"Well, anyway," she continued, "Mwari decided to make a master for all the animals.

VOCABULARY
stealthily—carefully; quietly.
sluggish current—slow moving flow of the water.
lunged—suddenly moved.
water lettuce—floating leaves.

"Escape" continued

He took clay from deep in Mother Earth's womb and formed a man. He had barely finished when Mother Earth said, 'My creator, this is a fine creature, but it looks like you, not me. Why don't you make another one?'

"Mwari took more clay and formed a woman. He took a little of the rivers and mountains, the grass and flowers, and added them to the clay to give Earth's beauty to the woman. He took a pinch of fire for her heart and a handful of water for her womb, so she could grow new life.

"When he was finished, he let his shadow fall over the pair. The animals had received only one spirit from Mother Earth, but the people had one from her and one from Mwari.

4. Who is Mwari, and why do you think Nhamo is telling this story?

STORY FRAME STORY FRAME

"Oh, why won't they go!" Nhamo cried out suddenly. "I'll die out here. My spirit will be trapped forever with those ugly animals watching me. I wish I'd never left home!"

She curled up into a ball. The water in the bottom of the boat soaked into her dress-cloth. It clung to her like a second, evil-smelling skin. She was alone, alone, alone and she was going to die.

Nhamo lay in a fit of grief with her eyes squeezed shut. But presently a breeze stirred the forest. The leaves tossed with a rushing sound and the scent of wild gardenias hidden somewhere in the trees blew from the shore. It was as if a hand stroked her hair—lightly, swiftly passing, but most certainly there. Nhamo opened her eyes.

Sometimes, when she was in the deserted village at dusk, the wind awoke as day shifted into night. It had a different quality from other breezes, just as the silvery air was different from the harsh light of noon. It seemed to have a voice, as of people talking far away, but she could never quite make out the words. She heard that voice now.

Nhamo . . . Nhamo . . ., it whispered. Or perhaps it only said *Aauuu*, the usual sound of the wind. Yet, if she strained her ears, she could almost hear it: *Nhamo . . .*

"Mother?" said Nhamo.

The wind blew away, riffling the water.

She sat up. The hippos were still floating in the central channel. The sun slanted through the trees, low and golden, sending showers of light around their drifting hulks. Something let go deep in Nhamo's spirit. She lay down again in the boat and fell into a sleep as profound as any she had had surrounded by the breathing of her cousins in the safety of the girls' hut.

VOCABULARY
gardenias—white flowers.
riffling—moving.
hulks—big bodies.
profound—deep.

5. How has Nhamo's problem been solved?

Return to your Anticipation Guide and respond to the statements again. Have you changed your mind about any of them?

III. GATHER YOUR THOUGHTS

A. ANALYZE A STORY. Think of the main story of Nhamo's journey in "Escape."

1. Write the characters, setting, and conflict in the Story Map below.
2. Then break up the story of what happens to Nhamo into 3 main events.

MAIN CHARACTERS	EVENT #1
SETTING	EVENT #2
CONFLICT	EVENT #3

STORY MAP

B. BRAINSTORM IDEAS Get ready to write a story about a frightening journey or escape. Use the web below to brainstorm story ideas.

WHO IS IT ABOUT?

WHY IS THERE A JOURNEY OR ESCAPE?

STORY TITLE:

WHERE DOES IT HAPPEN?

WHAT IS THE CONFLICT?

C. ORGANIZE A STORY Use the storyboards below to organize your story.

1. Begin your story right before the most exciting part.

2. Set the scene in the beginning, create a problem, and then solve the problem at the end.

1. THE SCENE

2. THE MAIN CHARACTER

3. THE PROBLEM

4. HOW THE CHARACTER FEELS

5. THE SOLUTION

IV. WRITE

Now draft your **story** in the space below.

1. Begin by setting the scene and introducing your main character.

2. Then introduce the problem or conflict and tell how it was solved.

3. Use the Writers' Checklist to help you revise.

Continue your writing on the next page.

Continue your writing from the previous page.

WRITERS'
CHECKLIST

COMMA SPLICES

☐ Did you avoid comma splices? A comma splice occurs when two simple sentences are joined with just a comma. EXAMPLE: *The tires spun, the car skidded to a stop.* To fix a comma splice, insert a comma plus a joining word (*and, or, but, so*) or a semicolon (;) between the sentences. EXAMPLE: *The tires spun; the car skidded to a stop.* Another option is to create two separate sentences.

WRAP-UP

What did you learn from reading Nhamo's story in "Escape"?

READERS'
CHECKLIST

MEANING

☐ Did you learn something from the reading?

☐ Did it affect you or make an impression?

20: Fear

Ask yourself a simple question: "What strikes fear in you?" For some people, it might be an angry parent or bullying classmate. In this memoir, Gary Soto looks at the word *fear* and describes what it feels like.

BEFORE YOU READ

Read the first and last paragraphs of "Fear."
1. Quickly skim the rest of the selection. Watch for the names of characters.
2. Look also for words that mean the same as *fear*. Note what you find in the boxes below.

IDEA IN FIRST PARAGRAPH

CHARACTERS' NAMES

WORDS OR PHRASES TO DESCRIBE *FEAR*

IDEA IN LAST PARAGRAPH

What do you think this story is about?

SKIMMING

As you read, ask yourself if any of Gary Soto's experiences remind you of your own.

1. Connect what's being described to your own feelings and experiences.

2. React to Soto's description of bullying by jotting down your own ideas and feelings about what happens.

EXAMPLE:
I never said anything to bullies either.

"Fear" from *Living up the Street* by Gary Soto

A cold day after school. Frankie T., who would drown his brother by accident that coming spring and would use a length of pipe to beat a woman in a burglary years later, had me pinned on the ground behind a <u>backstop</u>, his breath sour as meat left out in the sun. "<u>Cabrón</u>," he called me and I didn't say anything. I stared at his face, shaped like the sole of a shoe, and just went along with the insults, although now and then I tried to raise a shoulder in a halfhearted struggle because that was part of the game.

He let his <u>drool</u> yo-yo from his lips, missing my feet by only inches, after which he giggled and called me names. Finally he let me up. I slapped grass from my jacket and pants, and pulled my shirt tail from my pants to shake out the fistful of dirt he had stuffed in my collar. I stood by him, nervous and red-faced from struggling, and when he suggested that we climb the monkey bars together, I followed him quietly to the kid's section of Jefferson Elementary. He climbed first, with small

VOCABULARY
backstop—fence used to prevent a ball from going out of a playing area of a baseball diamond.
Cabron—Spanish for "crazy goat."
drool—saliva running from the mouth.

grunts, and for a second I thought of running but knew he would probably catch me—if not then, the next day. There was no way out of being a fifth grader—the daily event of running to teachers to show them your bloody nose. It was just a fact, like having lunch.

STOP AND RECORD

How would you describe Frankie? Write 3 words to describe him below.

RESPONSE NOTES

So I climbed the bars and tried to make conversation, first about the girls in our classroom and then about kickball. He looked at me smiling as if I had a camera in my hand, his teeth green like the underside of a rock, before he relaxed his grin into a simple gray line across his face. He told me to shut up. He gave me a hard stare and I looked away to a woman teacher walking to her car and wanted very badly to yell for help. She unlocked her door, got in, played with her face in the visor mirror while the engine warmed, and then drove off with blue smoke trailing. Frankie was watching me all along and when I turned to him, he laughed, "*Chale*! She can't help you, <u>ese</u>." He moved closer to me on the bars and I thought he was going to hit me; instead he put his arm around my shoulder, squeezing firmly in friendship. "C'mon, chicken, let's be cool."

VOCABULARY
ese—Spanish slang for "man."

I opened my mouth and tried to feel happy as he told me what he was going to have for Thanksgiving. "My Mamma's got a turkey and ham, lots of potatoes, yams and stuff like that. I saw it in the refrigerator. And she says, we gonna get some pies. Really, ese."

Poor liar, I thought, smiling as we clunked our heads softly like good friends. He had seen the same afternoon program on TV as I had, one in which a woman in an apron demonstrated how to prepare a Thanksgiving dinner. I knew he would have tortillas and beans, a round steak maybe and oranges from his backyard. He went on describing his Thanksgiving, then changed over to Christmas— the new bicycle, the clothes, the G.I. Joes. I told him that it sounded swell, even though I knew he was making it all up. His mother would in fact stand in line at the Salvation Army to come away hugging armfuls of toys that had been tapped back into shape by reformed alcoholics with veined noses. I pretended to be excited and asked if I could come over to his place to play after Christmas.

VOCABULARY

G.I. Joes—military action figure toys.
reformed alcoholics—men and women who once had a drinking problem but now do not.

"Fear" continued

What do you know about Frankie T.? Use this organizer to collect what you know.

WHAT THE CHARACTER SAYS	WHAT PEOPLE SAY ABOUT HIM
WHAT HE DOES	**HOW HE MAKES ME FEEL**

RESPONSE NOTES

"Oh yeah, anytime," he said, squeezing my shoulder and clunking his head against mine.

When he asked what I was having for Thanksgiving, I told him that we would probably have a ham with pineapple on the top. My family was slightly better off than Frankie's, though I sometimes walked around with cardboard in my shoes and socks with holes big enough to be ski masks, so holidays were extravagant happenings. I told him about the scalloped potatoes, the candied yams, the frozen green beans, and the pumpkin pie.

His eyes moved across my face as if he were deciding where to hit me—nose, temple, chin, talking mouth—and then he lifted his arm from my shoulder and jumped from the monkey bars, grunting as he landed. He wiped sand from his knees while looking up and

VOCABULARY
extravagant—big and important, filled with gifts.
scalloped—baked in milk or sauce.

warned me not to mess around with him any more. He stared with such a great meanness that I had to look away. He warned me again and then walked away. Incredibly <u>relieved</u>, I jumped from the bars and ran looking over my shoulder until I turned onto my street.

Frankie scared most of the school out of its wits and even had girls <u>scampering</u> out of view when he showed himself on the playground. If he caught us without notice, we grew quiet and stared down at our shoes until he passed after a threat or two. If he pushed us down, we stayed on the ground with our eyes closed and pretended that we were badly hurt. If he <u>riffled</u> through our lunch bags, we didn't say anything. He took what he wanted, after which we sighed and watched him walk away peeling an orange or chewing big chunks of an apple.

Still, that afternoon when he called Mr. Koligian, our teacher, a <u>foul</u> name—we grew scared for him. Mr. Koligian pulled and tugged at his body until it was in his arms and then out of his arms as he <u>hurled</u> Frankie against the building. Some of us looked away because it was unfair. We knew the house he lived in: The empty refrigerator, the father gone, the mother in a sad bathrobe, the beatings, the <u>yearnings</u> for something to love. When the

■ V O C A B U L A R Y ■
relieved—free from worry.
scampering—running quickly.
riffled—shuffled.
foul—bad; offensive.
hurled—threw.
yearnings—desires.

"Fear" continued

teacher <u>manhandled</u> him, we all wanted to run away, but instead we stared and felt shamed. Robert, Adele, Yolanda shamed; Danny, Alfonso, Brenda shamed; Nash, Margie, Rocha shamed. We all watched him flop about as Mr. Koligian shook and grew red from anger. We knew his house and, for some, it was the same one to walk home to: The broken mother, the <u>indifferent</u> walls, the refrigerator's glare which fed the people no one wanted.

VOCABULARY

manhandled—treated roughly.
indifferent—without emotion; uncaring.

STOP AND RECORD STOP AND RECORD STOP AND RECORD

What do you know about the narrator, Gary Soto? Use this organizer to collect your ideas.

WHAT HE SAYS

WHAT PEOPLE SAY ABOUT HIM

WHAT HE DOES

HOW HE MAKES ME FEEL

A. FORM AN OPINION An *opinion* is a person's thought or belief.

1. Read these statements about bullying.
2. Mark "T" for ones that you think are true.
3. Mark "F" for ones that you think are false.

TRUE/FALSE

	Bullying happens everywhere and can't be stopped.
	There will always be bullies, and there will always be victims.
	It's best to let kids work things out on their own.
	Bullies should be punished for their actions.
	Bullying can cause life-long unhappiness for the victims.
	People who are bullied usually get over it pretty quickly.
	Bullies often need as much sympathy as their victims.

B. SHAPE AN OPINION Plan to write an opinion paragraph about bullying.

1. Write a statement that tells your opinion about bullies. Write your own sentence or use one statement from above.
2. Then give 2 reasons that explain why you feel this way.

OPINION STATEMENT:

#1.

#2.

C. SUPPORT AN OPINION Writers support their opinions with facts, examples, personal experiences, and statements by experts.

1. Restate your opinion.

2. Then complete the organizer to show at least 3 different pieces of support for your opinion.

OPINION STATEMENT			
FACTS	EXAMPLES	PERSONAL EXPERIENCES	EXPERTS' STATEMENTS

WRITE

Now write a **paragraph of opinion**. Use notes from your organizer to help.

1. Start with a strong statement of your opinion.

2. Support your opinion with 2 or 3 facts, examples, personal experiences, or statements from experts.

3. Use the Writers' Checklist to help you revise.

Continue your writing on the next page.

WRITERS' CHECKLIST

APOSTROPHES

☐ Did you use apostrophes correctly to form the possessive of singular nouns? To show ownership, add an *'s* to singular nouns. EXAMPLES: *Katie's teacher, the woman's name, Chris's shirt*

☐ Did you use apostrophes correctly to form the possessive of plural nouns? Add only an apostrophe to plural nouns that end in *s*. EXAMPLES: *all the students' records, the cities' mayors* Add *'s* to plural nouns that do not end in *s*. EXAMPLES: *children's feelings, men's laughter*

V. WRAP-UP

What do you think is the point or main idea of "Fear"?

READERS' CHECKLIST

UNDERSTANDING

☐ Did you understand the reading?

☐ Was the message or point clear?

☐ Can you restate what the reading is about?

STOWAGE OF THE BRITISH SLAVE SHIP B

REGULATED SLAVE TRA

Act of 17

Fig
Longitudina

Slavery

Hold for Provisions, Water &c.

Note. The shaded Squares indicate the beams of the Ship.

PLAN OF LOWER DECK WITH THE STOWAGE

OF THESE BEING STOWED UNDER THE SHELVES AS SH

OWAGE OF 130 ADDITIONAL SLAVES ROUND THE WINGS OR SIDES OF THE LOW
ERIES IN A CHURCH) THE SLAVES STOWED ON THE SHELVES AND BELOW THE
BETWEEN THE BEAMS: AND FAR LESS UNDER TH

W O M E N   B O Y S

Starting in the 1500s, European countries brought West Africans to their colonies in the Americas to work as slaves. For the next 300 years, thousands of Africans were shipped across the Atlantic Ocean, destined for lives of labor and misery. While some slaves were more fortunate than others, all suffered the pain and humiliation of being owned.

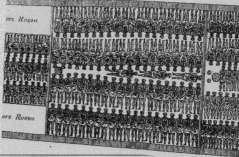

What do you know about slavery? How did it start? What was it like for the people who were enslaved? Personal accounts, like this one by Charles Ball, can help us understand the tragic events of more than 100 years ago.

BEFORE YOU READ

Use the K-W-L Chart to organize information about African-American slavery.

1. In the **K** column, write what you know about slavery.
2. Then write what you want to find out in the **W** column.
3. Save the **L** column for later, after you have finished reading.

K WHAT I KNOW

W WHAT I WANT TO KNOW

L WHAT I LEARNED

II. READ

Now read this true account of what it was like to be on a slave ship.

1. Mark or **highlight** information that helps you answer your questions from the K-W-L Chart.

2. In the Response Notes, write about how Ball's description makes you feel.

"Taken in Slavery" from *Slavery in the United States* by Charles Ball

At the time we came into this ship, she was full of black people, who were all confined in a dark and low place, in <u>irons</u>. The women were in irons as well as the men.

"About twenty persons were seized in our village, at the time I was; and amongst these were three children, so young that they were not able to walk, or to eat any hard <u>substance</u>. The mothers of these children had brought them all the way with them; and had them in their arms when we were taken on board this ship.

"When they put us in irons, to be sent to our place of <u>confinement</u> in the ship, the men who <u>fastened</u> the irons on these mothers, took the children out of their hands and threw them over the side of the ship, into the water. When this was done, two of the women leaped overboard after the children—the third was already confined by a chain to another woman, and could not get into the water, but in struggling to <u>disengage</u> herself she broke her arm, and died a few days after, of a fever. One of the two women

EXAMPLE:
Throwing children overboard makes me so angry and shocked.

VOCABULARY
irons—chains.
substance—food.
confinement—captivity, holding.
fastened—attached; locked.
disengage—free.

in the river was carried down by the weight of her irons, before she could be <u>rescued</u>; but the other was taken up by some men in a boat and brought on board. This woman threw herself overboard one night, when we were at sea.

STOP aND THINK

Why do the women throw themselves into the river?

_____

_____

_____

"The weather was very hot, whilst we lay in the river, and many of us died every day; but the number brought on board greatly <u>exceeded</u> those who died, and at the end of two weeks the place in which we were confined was so full that no one could lie down; and we were <u>obliged</u> to sit all the time, for the room was not high enough for us to stand. When our prison would hold no more, the ship sailed down the river, and on the night of the second day after she sailed, I heard the roaring of the ocean, as it dashed against her sides.

"After we had been at sea some days, the irons were removed from the women, and they

VOCABULARY
rescued—saved.
exceeded—outnumbered.
obliged—forced.

"Taken in Slavery" CONTINUED

were permitted to go upon deck; but whenever the wind blew high, they were driven down amongst us.

STOP aND THINK

What do you know about the person telling this story (the narrator)?

_____

_____

"We had nothing to eat but yams, which were thrown amongst us at random—and of these we had scarcely enough to support life. More than one-third of us died on the passage; and when we arrived at Charleston, I was not able to stand. It was more than a week after I left the ship, before I could straighten my limbs. I was bought by a trader, with several others; brought up the country, and sold to our present master: I have been here five years.

VOCABULARY
scarcely—hardly.
passage—way over.
Charleston—city and seaport in South Carolina that once was the center of the slave trade in the United States.
limbs—arms and legs.

STOP aND THINK

What made life on the slave ship so horrible?

_____

_____

_____

Now return to the **L** column of your K-W-L Chart. Write what you learned from Ball's memoir.

130 OF THESE BEING STOWED UNDER THE SHELVES AS SHEWN IN FIGURE D & FIGURE 5.

Store Room

GATHER YOUR THOUGHTS

A. ORGANIZE DETAILS Clustering can help you keep track of information. Use this cluster to organize details from "Taken in Slavery."

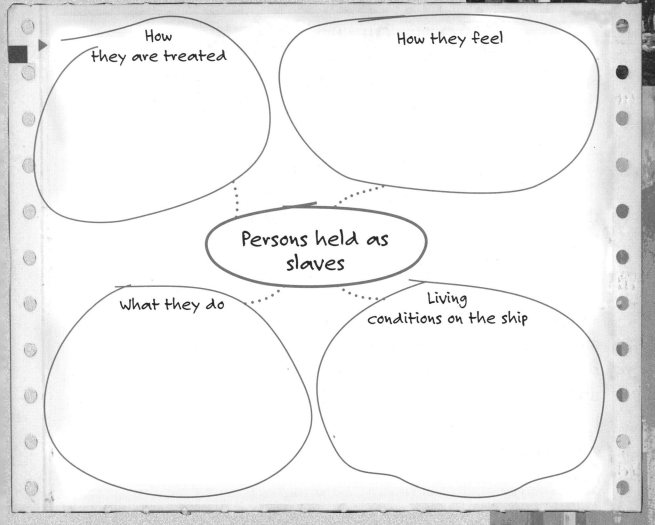

How
they are treated

How they feel

Persons held as
slaves

What they do

Living
conditions on the ship

B. PLAN Get ready to write a letter to Charles Ball. The purpose of your letter will be to tell him how you felt about his memoir.

1. FIRST WRITE A TOPIC SENTENCE.

2. THEN EXPLAIN WHY YOU FELT THIS WAY.
   REASON #1
   REASON #2
   REASON #3
3. SAY WHAT YOU LEARNED FROM READING HIS MEMOIR.

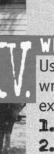

WRITE

Use your notes from the previous page to help you write a **letter** to Charles Ball. Your purpose is to explain how reading his memoir made you feel.

1. Begin with an overall statement of your feelings.
2. Then tell Mr. Ball why you feel this way. Give 2 or 3 reasons.
3. End by saying what you learned from his memoir.
4. Use the Writers' Checklist to help you revise.

Date

Dear

WRITERS' CHECKLIST

CONFUSING WORD PAIRS

❑ Did you use *bring* when the action is moving toward the speaker and *take* when the action is moving away?

EXAMPLE: *Please bring me a fork and take this spoon away!*

❑ Did you use *accept* as a verb to mean "to receive" and *except* as a preposition to mean "other than"?

EXAMPLE: *The night I accepted the award, everyone except my grandfather was there.*

Continue your writing on the next page.

Continue your writing from the previous page.

Sincerely yours,

V. WRAP-UP

What are some of the thoughts that "Taken in Slavery" stirred in you?

22: **Misery Days** and **A Child's Pain**

What do you know about long ago? What images and pictures come to mind when you think of slavery? Many writers try to help us remember our past so we will not forget the painful lessons it has taught us.

BEFORE YOU READ

Look carefully at the images and captions throughout "Misery Days" and "A Child's Pain."

1. Choose 2 photographs that interest you. Record your ideas about them in the chart below.

2. Then make a prediction about the selections.

PICTURE WALK

THE PHOTO OF...	TELLS ME...
#1	
#2	

I predict these selections will be about:

II. READ

In *To Be a Slave*, Julius Lester collects first-person stories from slaves. "Misery Days" and "A Child's Pain" are two of these accounts of slavery in the United States. Lester's comments are printed in italics.

1. Think of **questions** you would like to ask about slavery.
2. Write your questions, along with your ideas about possible answers, in the Response Notes.

A family seated in front of their ramshackle home

"Misery Days" by Julius Lester

The typical slave experience, however, was very different and was characterized by a vicious cruelty. Slaves were whipped for the most <u>trifling</u> incidents, and the whip was as often <u>wielded</u> by the slave owner's wife as the slave owner himself.

Whippings were also <u>administered</u> by the plantation overseer, a poor white, who was hired to watch the slaves while they worked, to make sure that they weren't lazy about the work and didn't try to run away. On the larger <u>plantations</u> a trusted slave would help the overseer. Known as the driver, he was used often by the owner or the overseer to give whippings. Sometimes a slave preferred to be whipped by the slave owner, because the driver would be more severe. Other drivers were more <u>lenient</u>.

EXAMPLE:
Did the driver get special privileges? — maybe better clothes or more food?

They whipped my father 'cause he looked at a slave they killed and cried.

ROBERTA MANSON
<u>Library of Congress</u>

VOCABULARY
trifling—unimportant; insignificant.
wielded—used.
administered—carried out.
plantations— the home and fields together, with the workers living on them, used for growing crops.
lenient— generous; less harsh.
Library of Congress—nation's library where the records of these slaves' words have been saved.

?? STOP aND QuesTiON ??

What would you like to ask Roberta Manson?

"Misery Days" CONTINUED

One day while my mammy was washing her back my sister noticed ugly <u>disfiguring</u> scars on it. <u>Inquiring</u> about them, we found, much to our amazement, that they were Mammy's <u>relics</u> of the now gone, if not forgotten, slave days. This was her first reference to her "misery days" that she had made in my presence. Of course we all thought she was telling us a big story and we made fun of her. With eyes flashing, she stopped bathing, dried her back and reached for the smelly ol' black whip that hung behind the kitchen door. <u>Bidding</u> us to strip down to our waists, my little mammy with the boney bent-over back, struck each of us as hard as ever she could with that black-snake whip. Each stroke of the whip drew blood from our backs. "Now," she said to us, "you have a taste of slavery days."

—FRANK COOPER
Library of Congress

RESPONSE NOTES

stop and clarify

Why does the mother whip her children?

VOCABULARY
disfiguring deforming.
Inquiring—asking.
relics—objects that have survived the passage of time.
Bidding—asking.

A family in the field picking cotton

"A Child's Pain" by Julius Lester

Occasionally a slave owner would try to be gentle with a child. Before purchasing the child, a few would attempt to make friends and persuade the child to come with them. This kind of concern, however, never <u>alleviated</u> the child's pain of being separated from its family.

Major Ellison bought me and carried me to Mississippi. I didn't want to go. They '<u>zamine</u> you just like they do a horse; they look at your teeth, and pull your eyelids back and look at your eyes, and feel you just like you was a horse. He 'zamined me and said, "Where's your mother?" I said, "I don't know where my mother is, but I know her." He said, "Would you know your mother if you saw her?" I said, "Yes, sir. I would know her. I don't know where she is, but I would know her." They had done sold her then. He said, "Do you want us to buy you?" I said, "No. I don't want you to buy me. I want to stay here." He said, "We'll be nice to you and give you plenty to eat." I said, "No, you won't have much to eat. What do you have to eat?" He said, "Lots of peas and cottonseed and things like that." But I said, "No, I'd rather stay here because I get plenty of pot licker and bread and buttermilk, and I don't want to go; I got plenty." I didn't know that that wasn't lots to eat.

A notice advertising slaves for sale

VOCABULARY
alleviated—helped or lessened.
'zamine—examine.

STOP AND PREDICT

Will Major Ellison return the girl to her mother? Explain your prediction.

_____

_____

"A Child's Pain" CONTINUED

He said, "Well, I have married your <u>mistress</u> and she wants me to buy you." But I still said, "I don't want to go." They had done sold my mother to Mr. Armstrong then. So he kept talking to me, and he said, "Don't you want to see your sister?" I said, "Yes, but I don't want to go there to see her." They had sold her to Mississippi before that, and I knowed she was there, but I didn't want to go.

I went on back home, and the next day the old white woman whipped me, and I said to myself, "I wish that old white man had bought me." I didn't know he had bought me anyhow, but soon they took my cotton dresses and put 'em in a box, and they combed my hair, and I heard them tell me that Mr. Ellison had done come after me and he was in a buggy. I wanted to ride in the buggy, but I didn't want to go with him. So when I saw him I had a bucket of water on my head, and I set it on the shelf and ran just as fast as I could for the woods. They caught me, and Aunt Bet said, "Honey, don't do that. Mr. Ellison done bought you and you must go with him." She tied my clothes up in a bundle and he had me sitting up in the buggy with him, and we

RESPONSE NOTES

Two men riding through the plantation

VOCABULARY

mistress—the person whom the girl was then working for.

"A Child's Pain" CONTINUED

started to his house here. I had to get down to open the gate, and when I got back up I got behind in the little seat for servants, and he told me to come back and get inside, but I said I could ride behind up to the house, and he let me stay there, but he kept watching me. He was scared I would run away, because I had done run away that morning, but I wasn't going to run away, 'cause I wouldn't know which way to go after I got that far away.

ANONYMOUS

[stop and summarize]

What frightened this young slave girl so much?

A family seated in a wagon

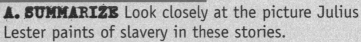

III. GATHER YOUR THOUGHTS

A. SUMMARIZE Look closely at the picture Julius Lester paints of slavery in these stories.
1. Go back and study carefully the 3 parts of this reading.
2. Then summarize what each part tells about slavery.

JULIUS LESTER'S COMMENTS	"MISERY DAYS"	"A CHILD'S PAIN"

B. REFLECT Prepare to write a reflective paragraph.
1. Look again at each part of the reading and ask yourself, "What have I learned from this?"
2. Write your answer in each box. Then write what you conclude from all of them.

WHAT I LEARNED

JULIUS LESTER'S COMMENTS	"MISERY DAYS"	"A CHILD'S PAIN"

CONCLUSION

Now write a **reflective paragraph**.
1. Begin by stating your overall reflection on the reading.
2. Then write a sentence reflecting on each of the 3 parts
of the reading.
3. Use the Writers' Checklist to help you revise.

WRITERS' CHECKLIST

SUBJECT/VERB AGREEMENT

☐ **Did you use singular verbs with *everybody*, *everyone*, *nobody* and *no one*? When one of these words is the subject of a sentence, the verb in the sentence must be singular.**
EXAMPLES: *Everyone is (not <u>are</u>) here. Nobody was (not <u>were</u>) alone.*

V. WRAP-UP

What did you learn from reading "Misery Days" and "A Child's Pain"?

READERS' CHECKLIST

MEANING

☐ **Did you learn something from the reading?**
☐ **Did it affect you or make an impression?**

Elizabeth Borton de Treviño

Elizabeth Borton de Treviño (1904–   ) has written many books for children. In 1966, Treviño won the Newbery Medal for *I, Juan de Pareja*, a fictional biography of the famous painter Velazquez and his black slave.

Born into Slavery

Do you like listening to stories? Listening to a story can make it easier for you to get involved in the plot and interested in the characters. It can also make it easier for you to go backward or forward in time so that you feel like you're there where the action is taking place.

BEFORE YOU READ

Choose a partner to help you read the selection aloud. Take turns reading the 2 paragraphs on the next page.

1. Visualize the people and places that are described.

2. Then make notes and sketches on the Listener's Log.

Listener's Log

DIRECTIONS Answer each question as best as you can. If you don't know an answer, make a guess.

WHERE AND WHEN DOES THE STORY TAKE PLACE?

WHO IS JUAN DE PAREJA?

WHAT DO YOU PREDICT THIS STORY WILL BE ABOUT?

MY SKETCH OF JUAN

MY SKETCH OF ZULEMA

READ

Take turns reading the rest of "Born into Slavery" aloud.
1. **Visualize** the people and places described.
2. Make sketches in the Response Notes of what you see.

"Born into Slavery" from *I, Juan de Pareja* by Elizabeth Borton de Treviño

I, Juan de Pareja, was born into slavery early in the seventeenth century. I am not certain of the year. My mother, who was called Zulema, was a very beautiful black woman, and though she never told me who my father was, I suspect that he was the keeper of one of our master's warehouses, a white Spaniard who could not afford to buy her. But I know that he did give her a golden <u>bracelet</u> and gold hoops for her ears.

She died when I was about five, and I was not told any more than that she had flown away to heaven. I have always wondered what happened. Perhaps my life might have been different if she had survived. It is likely that she died of a fever or some other illness. <u>Seville</u>, where we lived, was seldom without fear of the <u>plague</u>, for so many ships from foreign ports sailed up the <u>Guadalquivir</u> to tie at our docks, and anyone who died of a mysterious <u>malady</u> was <u>hastily</u> buried, in fear

EXAMPLE:

VOCABULARY
bracelet—band or chain, often of metal, worn around the wrist or arm.
Seville—city in southern Spain.
plague—deadly disease that is easily spread from person to person.
Guadalquivir—river in southern Spain.
malady—illness.
hastily—quickly.

and trembling and in the hope that he had not brought us the <u>pest</u>.

I missed my mother terribly, for she had always rocked me to sleep in her arms, even when I was a large child, and she sang to me softly in her deep rich <u>contralto</u>. Even now that I am an old man, and have come through so much, I can close my eyes and hear her voice humming the songs I loved, feel her arms around me, warm save for the pressure of her golden bracelet, and enjoy for a <u>fleeting</u> moment that sense of safety and of love with which she surrounded me.

Double-entry Journal

DIRECTIONS In the right-hand column, write your thoughts and feelings about the quote.

Quote	My Thoughts
"I missed my mother terribly, for she had always rocked me to sleep in her arms. . . ."	

She was a tender creature, <u>lavish</u> with small <u>caresses</u> and kindnesses. When she sat sewing on the mistress's <u>garments</u>, in the light of an eastern window in the early morning, she pierced the silks and velvets gently with her needle and smoothed the stuff with her <u>slender</u>, sensitive dark hands. Looking up at

VOCABULARY
pest—deadly disease.
contralto—low voice.
fleeting—passing.
lavish—very giving; generous.
caresses—soft, gentle touches.
garments—clothes.
slender—thin.

Respond to the quote.

Quote	My Thoughts

"Perhaps my life might have been different if she had survived."

"Born into Slavery" continued

me, she would smile, and her melting eyes would send love toward me, like a touch.

Ay, my mother. I have some knowledge of painting now, hard gained over the years of my life, and what a challenge to a painter you would have been! What a delight and a torment to try to catch the soft sheen of apple green taffeta and garnet velvet of the mistress's gown, the sober brown of yours, the pink and gold of your turban, picked up by the gold hoops in your ears and the beautiful dark glow, like that of a ripe purple grape, along your round cheek and slender neck. And how to paint your lovely hands, fluttering over the silks like two dark birds?

After my mother's death, the mistress took me for her page boy and dressed me in a fine suit of brilliant blue silk, and set an orange and silver turban on my head. Also, she gave me my mother's earrings, though she kept the bracelet and wore it. Mistress pierced my ear herself and drew a thread through the hole,

VOCABULARY
torment—mental pain.
sheen—shine.
taffeta—crispy, shiny fabric.
garnet velvet—deep red velvet, which is a soft, plush fabric or cloth.
sober—plain; simple.
turban—close-fitting hat made of material wound around a small inner cap.

moving it a bit each day until it healed, and then she hung one of the hoops in my ear.

"It cleans the blood to wear an earring," she told me. "There! I shall keep the other one for you, in case you lose this."

Mistress was kind but <u>capricious</u>, and she was often forgetful because she adored Master so much and he was always <u>ailing</u>, a constant worry to her. Mistress was a de Silva, of Portuguese descent, from the city of Oporto. It was my duty to walk behind her when she went out to the shops or to take <u>sherbet</u> with her friends, carrying her <u>reticule</u>, her fan, her <u>missal</u>, her <u>rosary</u> in its little pearl-studded box. "Juanico," she called me. "Juanico, my fan! No, do not hand it to me, fan me with it! I am suffocating with the heat. No, no, not so hard, you will muss my hair!"

I soon learned, with the <u>fatalism</u> of slave children, not to be surprised when she slapped me with her closed fan, a sharp rap that sent sudden pain along my hand and made tears sting under my eyelids. Just as suddenly, she might turn and set my turban straight and pinch my cheek fondly. I was in the same category as her little tan-and-white dog, Toto, which she <u>alternately cuffed and cuddled</u>.

VOCABULARY

capricious—likely to change suddenly without reason.
ailing—ill.
sherbet—frozen dessert that is sweet and cold.
reticule—handbag.
missal—Catholic prayer book.
rosary—string of beads on which prayers are counted.
fatalism—idea that events are predetermined and can't be changed.
alternately cuffed and cuddled—sometimes hit or slapped and sometimes held gently.

"Born into Slavery"

Yet I was devoted to Mistress. When I was sick she watched over me and got up in the night to bring me <u>broth</u>. She saw that I had clean water to wash in, and she gave me a piece of her own soap each time she ordered the long white bars for her bath. She fed me well and saw that I had money to buy sweets in the street, and sometimes she let me go to watch the strolling players or to the fair.

Double-entry Journal

Write your thoughts about this quote.

Quote	My Thoughts
"I soon learned, with the fatalism of slave children, not to be surprised when she slapped me with her closed fan. . . ."	

I will always be grateful to her for one thing—she taught me my <u>letters</u>. My mistress, I realize now, like many women of her class, had very little education. She read slowly and <u>laboriously</u>, and it always took her several tearful afternoons to <u>compose</u> a letter to her family in Portugal or to her nephew in Madrid, a young man who was a painter. Yet Mistress had a great deal of practical wisdom, and she knew many things because she trusted her judgment and <u>cultivated</u> her memory.

VOCABULARY
broth—light, almost clear kind of soup.
letters—knowledge of books.
laboriously with hard work.
compose—write.
cultivated—improved.

"Born into Slavery" continued

One hot afternoon in September she called me to her bedroom, and for once she did not begin immediately to list a series of errands and duties for me to perform. She was wearing a <u>gauzy</u> cool dress for, although she had drawn the curtains to keep out the sun and to preserve the colors of her <u>Moorish</u> carpet, the room was warm and her forehead was damp. She was fanning herself, gasping a little.

"Stand over there, Juanico," she said. "I wish to study you." She took a long, steady look at me. Then she nodded her head. "Yes," she said to herself. "Yes, I believe he is intelligent enough. Quite."

Then she spoke to me, mopping her neck with a large white cotton handkerchief.

"I am going to teach you the alphabet," she told me. "If you pay attention and practice well, you will learn to write a fair hand, and then you will be able to do my letters for me, and perhaps later on help Master at the warehouse. I will arrange that nobody is to bother you while I am having my afternoon <u>siesta</u>; in those hours you are to practice."

Double-entry Journal

Write your ideas about the quote.

Quote	My Thoughts
"I will always be grateful to her for one thing—she taught me my letters."	

V O C A B U L A R Y
gauzy—thin and nearly see-through.
Moorish—Arabic.
siesta—nap.

III. GATHER YOUR THOUGHTS

A. CREATE A CHARACTER "Born into Slavery" introduces readers to 3 interesting characters—Juan, his mother, and his mistress. Make up an interesting character of your own.

1. Imagine a person who lived long ago.

2. Fill in the web below with details.

PERSONALITY

AGE

APPEARANCE

My character

BELIEFS

HABITS

B. DEVELOP A CHARACTER Now get ready to write a character sketch. Name your character and use the organizer to tell more about him or her.

HOW HE OR SHE LOOKS

HOW OTHERS FEEL ABOUT HIM OR HER

CHARACTER'S NAME

HOW HE OR SHE ACTS

WHERE HE OR SHE LIVES

HOW HE OR SHE FEELS

IV. WRITE

Write a **character sketch** of the person you imagined.

1. Have the character introduce himself or herself as Juan does in the opening line of "Born into Slavery."
2. Then the character should give information about the time and place in which he or she lived.
3. Use the Writers' Checklist to help you revise.

V. WRAP-UP

What did you think was most interesting
about "Born into Slavery"?

READERS' CHECKLIST

ENJOYMENT

☐ Did you like the reading?

☐ Was the reading experience pleasurable?

☐ Would you want to reread the piece or recommend it to someone?

24: My Master

Have you ever seen great artists or craftspeople at work? They have perfected a skill by working at it day after day. Writers and readers, too, acquire their skills through daily practice.

I. BEFORE YOU READ

Get together with a partner. Carefully read and study each sentence in the "Think-Pair-Share" below.

1. Put a 1 before the sentence that you think comes first in the story, a 2 before the sentence that comes next, and so on. Share your answers.

2. Then write your prediction on what "My Master" is about.

Think-Pair-Share

_____ "'THESE ARE PROFESSIONAL SECRETS. KEEP THEM IN YOUR HEAD.'"

_____ "ONCE PROPERLY STRETCHED ON THE FRAME, THE CLOTH HAD TO BE PREPARED TO TAKE THE PAINT."

_____ "MUCH LATER, I HAD TO LEARN TO STRETCH COTTON CANVAS TO THE FRAMES, AND WHEN I HAD LEARNED THE TRICK OF IT, I WAS SET TO DOING THE SAME WITH LINEN."

_____ "FIRST, I HAD TO LEARN TO GRIND THE COLORS."

_____ "MY CORNERS DIDN'T FIT, OR THE SIDE PIECES WERE NOT PRECISELY TO MEASUREMENT, OR THE PEGS WERE TOO CLUMSY."

What will this story be about?

_____

_____

_____

_____

READ

Now read "My Master," which tells more of the story of Juan begun in "Born into Slavery."

1. As you read, think about what you like and dislike about the story.

2. Clarify words or phrases that you think are especially effective or interesting.

"My Master" from *I, Juan de Pareja* by Elizabeth Borton de Treviño

However, I soon found that I was not to do anything but serve Master, and he did not even want me to help him dress or to lay out his clothes. I brushed them and rubbed oil into his belts and boots, but Mistress herself, like a good wife (and I suspect because she adored him, and loved to work over and touch his things), sewed and mended his linen and saw that it was fresh. Master had other plans for me.

He had allowed me to rest and heal in those first days in his home. As soon as I was well, he said, "Come," and he took me into his studio.

EXAMPLE:
Excellent sentence—It builds suspense.

stop+predict

What do you think Juan's job will be in the studio?

....

....

stop+predict

This was a large room on the second floor of the house. It was almost <u>bare</u>, with a great window to the north that let in a pure cold light.

VOCABULARY
bare—empty.

Several easels, strong and sturdy, stood about, a chair or two, and there was a long table with a palette on it, a vase full of brushes, rags, and bits of canvas and wood for frames. In winter the studio was bitter cold, and in summer it was hot as an oven. During the heat it was full of smells, as well, for with the windows flung wide open, there ascended to us from the street the odor of refuse, of horse dung, and of tanning leather, for there was a leather craftsman near by. The smells were awful, but Master never noticed anything . . . heat nor cold nor bad smells nor dust. All he thought about was light, and the only days when he was nervous were days of low fog or rain that changed the light he lived by.

One by one, he taught me my duties. First, I had to learn to grind the colors. There were many mortars for this work, and pestles in varying sizes. I soon learned that the lumps of earth and metallic compounds had to be softly and continuously worked until there remained a powder as fine as the ground rice ladies used on their cheeks and foreheads. It took hours, and sometimes when I was sure the stuff was as fine as satin, Master would pinch and move it between his sensitive fingers, and

VOCABULARY
easels—upright frames.
palette—board that an artist holds while painting and on which colors are mixed.
canvas—heavy fabric on which things are painted.
ascended—rose.
refuse—trash.
dung—manure.
mortars—grinding tools.
pestles—club-shaped tools for grinding.
compounds—substances.

"My Master" continued

shake his head, and then I had to grind some more. Later the ground powder had to be <u>incorporated</u> into the oils, and well-mixed, and much later still, I arranged Master's palette for him, the little mounds of color each in its fixed place, and he had his preferences about how much of any one should be set out.

stop+predict

Will Juan's master be kind or cold-hearted? Why?

....

....

....

stop+predict

And, of course, brushes were to be washed daily, in plenty of good <u>Castile</u> soap and water. Master's brushes all had to be clean and fresh every morning when he began to work.

Much later, I had to learn to stretch cotton canvas to the frames, and when I had learned the trick of it, I was set to doing the same with linen. This was, for me, the hardest <u>task</u> of all.

Master had all the tools for framing the canvas sharpened and put into good order and bought me plenty of wood to practice with. Each time I built a frame and stretched a canvas, holding the frame <u>taut</u> with wooden pins, and nailing the canvas on around the frame, he showed me the flaws in my work by his expression. For some time the trouble was

VOCABULARY
incorporated—mixed.
Castile—Spanish.
task—work.
taut—straight; tight.

with my carpentry. My corners didn't fit, or the side pieces were not <u>precisely</u> to measurement, or the pegs were too clumsy. Oh, it took care and thought, and I shed many tears. Doña Emilia had never asked more of me than to fan her or hand her a sweet or hold her <u>parasol</u>, until she taught me to write. But this work was a man's, and I <u>grieved</u> that I could not learn it.

stop+clarify

What is Juan's master training him to become?

One day when I had failed for the third time at trying to fit a frame on which he wanted to stretch a good linen canvas, Master put down his palette, left his model fretting on the model stand, and showed me just how. His fingers were slim and sensitive, with dark hairs on the second knuckle; his nails were almond-shaped. Many a woman would have been proud to have such delicate hands as his. He cut and fitted the pieces precisely, so easily, so quickly, that I lost heart. I had <u>spoiled</u> so many. I put my head in my hands and sobbed.

VOCABULARY
precisely—exactly.
parasol—umbrella used for shielding a person from the sun.
grieved—felt sad and frustrated.
spoiled—ruined.

stop+think

How can you tell Juan enjoys his work?

stop+think

"My Master" continued

He lifted my head at once, smiled briefly, a mere flash of white teeth under the small dark mustache, and hurried back to his easel. I took the wood and the tool, held them just as he had and tried again, and this time it came right. I never failed again, and from then on I stretched all his canvases.

But this was but the beginning. Once properly stretched on the frame, the cloth had to be prepared to take the paint. We had many coatings we put on; Master taught me all the <u>formulae</u> from memory. In an excess of <u>enthusiasm</u>, I told Master I could write and that I would note down all the preparations.

"No," he said. "These are professional secrets. Keep them in your head."

stop+reflect

How would you describe Juan's life?

stop+reflect

VOCABULARY
formulae—ways; methods.
enthusiasm—excitement.

GATHER YOUR THOUGHTS

A. REACT TO LITERATURE Get ready to write a paragraph about "My Master." Consider the characters, setting, plot, writing style, and theme.

1. Make notes about the parts of the story in the organizer.
2. Give your opinion of how much you liked "My Master." Circle the number that best describes your reaction.

| 1 | 2 | 3 | 4 | 5 | 6 | 7 | 8 | 9 | 10 |

liked a little   liked a lot

"My Master"

CHARACTER

SETTING

PLOT

WRITING STYLE

THEME

B. SUPPORT AN OPINION Now complete the organizer to plan the 3 parts of your paragraph about "My Master."

OVERALL OPINION:

REASONS AND EVIDENCE:
1.
2.
3.

CONCLUSION:

IV. WRITE

Write your **paragraph about literature** below.

1. Start with a topic sentence that states your point of view about "My Master."
2. Then write at least 3 reasons to support your point of view.
3. End with a sentence that restates your opinion.
4. Use the Writers' Checklist for help revising.

Continue your writing on the next page.

Continue your writing from the previous page.

V. WRAP-UP

Did you find "My Master" easy or hard to read? Why?

READERS' CHECKLIST

EASE

- ❑ Was the passage easy to read?
- ❑ Were you able to read it smoothly and without difficulty?

Acknowledgments

8 "How Things Work," by Gary Soto. Copyright © 1985. Used by permission of the author.

10 "Proving Myself," by Eve Bunting. Excerpt from YOUR MOVE, copyright © 1998 by Eve Bunting, reprinted and recorded by permission of Harcourt, Inc.

13 "Mrs. Olinski," from THE VIEW FROM SATURDAY, by E. L. Konigsberg. Reprinted with permission of Ateneum Books for Young Readers, an imprint of Simon & Schuster Children's Publishing Division from THE VIEW FROM SATURDAY by E. L. Konigsburg. Copyright © 1996 E. L. Konigsburg

22 "The Day It Rained Cockroaches," from THE PIGMAN AND ME, by Paul Zindel. Copyright © 1991 by Paul Zindel.

33 "Eyewitness to the Boston Tea Party," from THE NIGHT THE REVOLUTION BEGAN by Wesley Griswold. Copyright © 1972 by Wesley Griswold.

41 "Lexington and Concord," from THE AMERICAN REVOLUTION, by Bruce Bliven, Jr. Copyright © 1958 and renewed 1986 by Bruce Bliven, Jr. Reprinted by permission of Random House, Inc.

51 "Ready," from JOHNNY TREMAIN, by Esther Forbes. Copyright © 1943 by Esther Forbes Hoskins and © renewed 1971 by Linwood M. Erskine, Jr., Executor of the Estate of Esther Forbes Hoskins. Reprinted by permission of (H. M.) Co. All rights reserved.

60 "It's Tonight," from JOHNNY TREMAIN, by Esther Forbes. Copyright © 1943 by Esther Forbes Hoskins and © renewed 1971 by Linwood M. Erskine, Jr., Executor of the Estate of Esther Forbes Hoskins. Reprinted by permission of (H. M.) Co. All rights reserved.

71 "Hanging Out," from RUMBLE FISH, by S. E. Hinton. Copyright © 1975 by Susan Eloise Hinton. Used by permission of Delacorte Press, a division of Random House, Inc.

76 "Being Fourteen," from CAN YOU SUE YOUR PARENTS FOR MALPRACTICE?, by Paula Danziger. Copyright © 1979 by Paula Danziger.

85 "Attack," from DEAR AMERICA: THE GIRL WHO CHASED AWAY SORROW. THE DIARY OF SARAH NITA, A NAVAHO GIRL, by Ann Turner. Copyright © 1999 by Ann Turner. Reproduced by permission of Scholastic, Inc.

105, 111 "The Washwoman," from IN MY FATHER'S COURT, by Isaac Bashevis Singer. Copyright © 1962 by Isaac Bashevis Singer.

123 "Louie Hirshfield," from THE ZODIACS, by Jay Neugeboren. Copyright © 1969 by Jay Neugeboren. Reprinted by permission of The Richard Parks Agency.

132 "George Santini," from THE ZODIACS, by Jay Neugeboren. Copyright © 1969 by Jay Neugeboren. Reprinted by permission of The Richard Parks Agency.

143 "You Can't Swallow Me Up," by Tomás Rivera, is reprinted with permission from the publisher of . . . Y NO SE LO TRAGÓ LA TIERRA . . . AND THE EARTH DID NOT DEVOUR HIM, translated by Evangelina Vigil-Piñon. Houston: Arte Publico Press—University of Houston, 1987.

152 "Migrant Family Life," from DARK HARVEST: MIGRANT FAMILY LIFE IN AMERICA, by Brent Ashabranner, with photographs by Paul Conklin (North Haven, Conn: Linnet Books, 1993). Text © 1985 by Brent Ashabranner. Reprinted by permission.

163 "September 3, 1919," from LETTERS FROM RIFKA, by Karen Hesse. Copyright © 1992 by Karen Hesse.

171 "October 5, 1919," from LETTERS FROM RIFKA, by Karen Hesse. Copyright © 1992 by Karen Hesse.

181 "Escape," from A GIRL NAMED DISASTER, by Nancy Farmer. Copyright © 1996 by Nancy Farmer. Reprinted by permission of the publisher. Orchard Books. New York. All rights reserved.

194 "Fear," from LIVING UP THE STREET, by Gary Soto. Copyright © 1985. This excerpt is used by permission of the author.

212, 214 "Misery Days" and "A Child's Pain" from TO BE A SLAVE, by Julius Lester. Copyright © 1968 by Julius Lester. Used by permission of Dial Books for Young Readers, a division of Penguin Putnam Inc.

221 "Born into Slavery," from "One: In which I learn my letters" from I, JUAN DE PAREJA; by Elizabeth Borton de Treviño. Copyright © 1965 by Elizabeth Borton de Treviño. Copyright renewed 1993 by Elizabeth Borton de Treviño. Reprinted by permission of Farrar, Straus and Giroux, LLC.

221 "My Master," from "Four: In which I learn my duties" from I, JUAN DE PAREJA; by Elizabeth Borton de Treviño. Copyright © 1965 by Elizabeth Borton de Treviño. Copyright renewed 1993 by Elizabeth Borton de Treviño. Reprinted by permission of Farrar, Straus and Giroux, LLC.

Photography:

COVER: All photos © Eileen Ryan.

TABLE OF CONTENTS and INTRODUCTION: All photos © Eileen Ryan except where noted. 3: center—courtesy Library of Congress. 4: upper right—courtesy Library of Congress. 5: center left—courtesy Library of Congress. 8: bottom—courtesy Library of Congress.

CHAPTER 1: All photos © Eileen Ryan except where noted. 11: lower right—courtesy Library of Congress. 13: © Jon Riley / Tony Stone Images. 22: upper right—courtesy Library of Congress. 24: lower left—courtesy Library of Congress. 26: bottom—courtesy Library of Congress. 27: bottom—courtesy Library of Congress. 29: top—courtesy Library of Congress.

CHAPTER 2: All photos courtesy Library of Congress except where noted. 32: background—© Eileen Ryan. 34: © Eileen Ryan. 35-36, 38-39, backgrounds—© Eileen Ryan.

CHAPTER 3: All photos courtesy Library of Congress.

CHAPTER 4: All photos © Eileen Ryan except where noted. 78: bottom—courtesy Library of Congress.

Acknowledgments continued

CHAPTER 5: All photos courtesy Library of Congress.

CHAPTER 6: All photos courtesy Library of Congress except where noted. 104–105, 110, 113, 115, 117: bottom—© Eileen Ryan. 120: top—© Eileen Ryan.

CHAPTER 7: All photos courtesy Library of Congress except where noted. 124: bottom—© Eileen Ryan. 128–129, 131, 132, 133, 134, 135, 137, 138–139: © Eileen Ryan.

CHAPTER 8: All photos courtesy Library of Congress.

CHAPTER 9: All photos courtesy Library of Congress.

CHAPTER 10: All photos © Eileen Ryan except where noted. 179: top and bottom—courtesy Library of Congress. 185–186: courtesy Library of Congress. 187: courtesy NASA. 188: bottom—courtesy Library of Congress. 194: top—courtesy Library of Congress. 196: courtesy Library of Congress.

CHAPTER 11: All photos courtesy Library of Congress except where noted. 203, 206, 209, 210, 211, 214, 216, 218: backgrounds—© Eileen Ryan.

CHAPTER 12: All photos © Eileen Ryan except where noted. 219: bottom—courtesy Library of Congress. 220, 236–237: courtesy Library of Congress.

Cover and Book Design: Christine Ronan and Sean O'Neill, Ronan Design

Permissions:
Feldman and Associates

Developed by Nieman Inc.

The editors have made every effort to trace the ownership of all copyrighted selections found in this book and to make full acknowledgment for their use. Omissions brought to our attention will be corrected in a subsequent edition.

Author/Title Index